COACHING IN ISLAMIC CULTURE

The Professional Coaching Series
Series Editor: David A. Lane

Other titles in the series

The Art of Inspired Living: Coach Yourself with Positive Psychology
Sarah Corrie

Integrated Experiential Coaching: Becoming an Executive Coach
Lloyd Chapman, with contributing author Sunny Stout Rostron

Coaching in the Family Owned Business: A Path to Growth
edited by Manfusa Shams and David A. Lane

Coaching in Education: Getting Better Results for Students, Educators, and Parents
edited by Christian van Nieuwerburgh

Internal Coaching: The Inside Story
Katharine St John-Brooks

Business Coaching International: Transforming Individuals and Organizations (Second Edition)
Sunny Stout-Rostron

Swings and Roundabouts: A Self-Coaching Workbook for Parents and Those Considering Becoming Parents
Anna Golawski, Agnes Bamford, and Irvine Gersch

Coaching on the Axis: Working with Complexity in Business and Executive Coaching
Marc Simon Kahn

Supporting the Family Business: A Coaching Practitioner's Handbook
Manfusa Shams and David A. Lane

The Cross-Cultural Coaching Kaleidoscope: A Systems Approach to Coaching Amongst Different Cultural Influences
Jennifer Plaister-Ten

COACHING IN ISLAMIC CULTURE
The Principles and Practice of Ershad

*Christian van Nieuwerburgh
and Raja'a Yousif Allaho*

Routledge
Taylor & Francis Group
LONDON AND NEW YORK

First published 2017 by Karnac Books Ltd.

Published 2018 by Routledge
2 Park Square, Milton Park, Abingdon, Oxon OX14 4RN
711 Third Avenue, New York, NY10017, USA

Routledge is an imprint of the Taylor & Francis Group, an informa business

Copyright © 2017 by Christian van Nieuwerburgh and Raja'a Yousif Allaho

The rights of Christian van Nieuwerburgh and Raja'a Yousif Allaho to be identified as the authors of this work have been asserted in accordance with §§ 77 and 78 of the Copyright Design and Patents Act 1988.

British Library Cataloguing in Publication Data

A C.I.P. for this book is available from the British Library

ISBN-13: 9781782201991 (pbk)

Typeset by Medlar Publishing Solutions Pvt Ltd, India

To

My mother, a role model of resilience and kindness
Cathia and Christian, who inspire me daily
And the memory of my father

Christian

To

My father, the role model in my life
My sons, Yousef and Fahad, my life project
And the memory of my mother

Raja'a

CONTENTS

ACKNOWLEDGEMENTS   ix

ABOUT THE AUTHORS   xi

SERIES EDITOR'S FOREWORD   xiii

FOREWORD   xvii

INTRODUCTION   xxi

CHAPTER ONE
A brief history of coaching   1

CHAPTER TWO
Coaching in Islamic culture   9

CHAPTER THREE
Listening with purpose   21

CHAPTER FOUR
Asking powerful questions   37

CHAPTER FIVE
Summarising and paraphrasing   47

CHAPTER SIX
Giving and receiving feedback   57

CHAPTER SEVEN
Ershad coaching framework   67

CHAPTER EIGHT
The Alignment Wheel   89

CHAPTER NINE
The coaching way of being   103

CHAPTER TEN
Conclusion   111

CHAPTER ELEVEN
Case studies and personal stories   117

REFERENCES   145

INDEX   149

ACKNOWLEDGEMENTS

We are grateful to Oliver Rathbone, Rod Tweedy, and Professor David Lane for believing in us and commissioning this book. Our efforts were made easier through the enthusiastic support of wonderful colleagues at Karnac: Kate Pearce, Cecily Blench, and Alex Massey.

The insights and stories of our case study authors have added richness to the text. We want to thank Jan Alen, Helen Ashley, Esther Chater, Charmaine Klima, Ronnie Zachary Nganwa, Mohammed Salah Salih, Aneta Tunariu, and Annette Wilson. We were particularly inspired by the personal story shared by Rania Shamas who has been very support-ive of this project.

Throughout this process, we have the good fortune to be able to put our ideas to trusted colleagues who have kindly shared their thoughts with us: John Campbell, Professor Irvine Gersch, Professor Peter Hawkins, Ajaz Hussain, Martin Jalili, Dr Ali Q. Jawad, Professor Stephen Joseph, Imam Feisal Abdul Rauf, Denis Sartain, Dr Aneta Tunariu, and Professor Mary Watt.

We both enjoy the work we do and we wish to appreciate and thank all of our clients. We have been developing this concept while work-ing with leaders, executives, and educators in Abu Dhabi, Dubai,

Kuwait, Lebanon, Qatar, and Saudi Arabia. Their ideas, responses, and insights have informed the writing of this book.

Finally, we want to recognise how much we have appreciated each other in this writing process. Both of us have felt honoured and privileged to work with the other. We have both learned so much from the opportunity to work together. We hope that we have been able to present something helpful and inspiring.

ABOUT THE AUTHORS

Dr Christian van Nieuwerburgh is professor of coaching and positive psychology at the University of East London in the UK. He is a highly sought-after executive coach, researcher, and consultant. Christian is particularly interested in interculturally-sensitive coaching, the creation of coaching cultures, and the use of coaching and positive psychology within educational settings. He publishes extensively in the field of coaching and is the author of *An Introduction to Coaching Skills: A Practical Guide* (Sage, 2017) and the editor of *Coaching in Education: Getting Better Results for Students, Educators and Parents* (Karnac, 2012) and *Coaching in Professional Contexts* (Sage, 2016). Christian is also director of research for Growth Coaching International, a specialist coach training provider for the education sector. Seen as a thought leader within the fields of coaching and positive psychology, he regularly speaks at conferences in Europe, the US, Australia, and the Middle East.

Raja'a Yousif Allaho is an executive coach, speaker, trainer, and writer. She has over twenty years of experience in the provision of consultancy, training, and coaching, specialising in people development and performance. She is a proficient certified coach and trainer with extensive experience of providing coaching and training services for managers and executives. Combining international knowledge with local cultural context, she successfully supports executives to achieve their targets and aspirations. She works primarily in the oil, government, telecommunications, and banking sectors. Raja'a is the founder and leader of Mashar Coaching School, the first bilingual coaching school in the Middle East where she has trained, coached, and mentored more than 120 professional coaches. As a master trainer of personal development assessment tools and methodologies, Raja'a is certified by a number of international companies.

SERIES EDITOR'S FOREWORD

Coaching through values to reach a higher purpose

In commissioning this volume as part of our professional coaching series we were aware that much of the debate in the field has been dominated by Western humanistic philosophy.

We have previously sought to give a voice to intercultural and cross-culturally informed practice in the work of several of our authors. Hence, work on international business coaching has addressed issues of culture and diversity and contributors on family business coaching have explored varied family and cultural business traditions. Recently we published a kaleidoscope model to work across cultures.

However, largely (although not entirely) missing from the coaching literature have been significant attempts to build models consistent with specific religious or cultural traditions.

Our authors Christian and Raja'a have attempted the task of filling that gap. Working from source material in Islamic scholarship they have set out to identify those features in Islamic teaching that provide a purpose consistent with its value base that also enable a coaching journey.

The model they have developed, the "Ershad coaching framework", provides a new and significant addition to our understanding of the power of coaching and the way journeys of discovery can emerge within specific spiritual traditions.

I am pleased that Imam Feisal Abdul Rauf has read and endorsed the book. His scholarly reflections enable the reader to understand how this fits within an Islamic culture but also he reaches out across religions to seek connections that bind us all. As he has so eloquently spoken to the book from that perspective I will seek to place it within the broader coaching literature.

Our authors have started this text by outlining some of the traditions that have underpinned coaching in Western cultures. Taking the story of Mentor as the starting point we have the idea of a wise guide helping a dissolute youth find his or her true self by setting a series of tasks but also directly intervening as needed. This positioning also finds expression in the role played by former champion athletes helping competitors in the original Olympic Games. It is this pattern that found its way into later uses of coaching in sports and education—the older and wiser person with core content knowledge assisting the younger to reach performance targets that could be directly measured.

Recently the role of coach as guide or facilitator of a journey of discovery has emerged. In this perspective the coach does not necessarily hold expert content knowledge that he or she can impart but rather uses an understanding of how to enable the journey the client wants to undertake. This draws on a different set of assumptions and skills.

In the Ershad coaching framework presented in this book, the authors propose three elements for effective coaching: a set of skills; a conversational process; and a coaching way of being. These are consistent with current facilitative approaches to coaching but they draw upon long-held Islamic precepts to underpin each of these that predate modern psychology.

The concept of a way of being is central to the work of the effective coach. The coach brings:

1. Compassion and gentleness
2. Patience
3. Humanity, and is willing to support all people, accepting everyone without discrimination.

These concepts are expanded in the book to provide the underpinning to practice.

The authors recommend that facilitators of Ershad will show these characteristics in varied areas of their practice, including deep interest in clients' growth, empathy and compassion, patience when working with their learners, being trustworthy, and promoting humanity and equality.

The connections that are sought between a coaching model built on Islamic teaching and principles and practices from Western traditions enable the reader to negotiate the terrain without fear and find ways to reflect upon and learn from different traditions.

This is an important book—a significant contribution and one I am delighted to welcome to our growing series. The intention is to publish this in English and in due course Arabic and in doing so we hope to enable conversations between scholars in coaching drawing upon very different philosophies. It is also a very practical book that in the hands of a skilled coach will enable clients to develop journeys to discovery that feel coherent with their values. As such it is not just for those working within Islamic cultures but for all coaches interested in how a values base can underpin a coaching framework.

I commend it to all our readers who I am sure will learn much to inform their own coaching practice.

Series Editor
Professor David A. Lane
Professional Development Foundation

FOREWORD

"God loves those of you who whenever they do something, excel in doing it," said the Prophet Muhammad.

With this book, professional coaches Christian van Nieuwerburgh and Raja'a Yousif Allaho supply a method for all within the Muslim world and beyond to live life more fully, whether at work or home. The coaching profession, as we know it today, is commonly regarded as Western, but the authors, who hail respectively from Belgium and Kuwait, illustrate by their collaboration how cross-cultural coaching is and can be.

Good is universal. Many modern Muslims falsely believe the myth that much of what we learn from other cultures is "un-Islamic", forgetting that the apogee of Islamic civilisation occurred precisely because the Prophet Muhammad urged his followers to seek knowledge "even as far as China", and added that "Knowledge is the lost inheritance of the believer; wherever he finds it, he should claim it." Many modern Muslims are unaware that the famous Islamic jurisprudential work *al-Mustasfa* of Imam al-Ghazali is based on an application of Greek philosophy, which the Muslims had acquired from the Greeks.

Muslims' absorption of Indian mathematics enabled them to invent algebra (*al-jabr*), and the Muslim mathematician al-Khwarizm created what became named after him, *algorithm* and *logarithm*.

Coaching, however, is not alien to Islam, although perhaps expressed in differing vocabulary. This is the task of our authors, to show how readily Islamic thought and spirituality accommodate and already instance the key concepts, practices, and values of coaching.

Coaching, most concisely defined, is facilitated self-guidance towards reaching goals. A practice emerging from the social sciences, especially psychology, coaching is, like all scientific methods, open to all—a notion for which the authors credit the medieval philosopher al-Ghazali.

For many of us, quandaries over careers have become so challenging today, especially as they intersect with other life commitments, that we need help identifying our own goals. The coach facilitates a partnership with a self-learner. The coach listens for the range of advice learners already have for themselves, implicit in what they say, and helps nudge it towards the light of their consciousness. The qualities needed to perform this service, such as empathy, humility, patience, respect, and intellect are already Muslim values. If, as the authors write, coaching is a one-to-one conversation embedded in a partnership, we need not look far for analogies in the Qur'an and Sunnah, and our spiritual, intellectual, and cultural heritage, which this book amply supplies.

Ershad, meaning "guidance", is the Arabic term the authors have taken to name their Muslim method of coaching, probably because the *murshid* (guide) is the traditional name given to the spiritual guide who provides one-on-one guidance to evolve the spiritual seeker to his or her highest spiritual state. Analogously, Ershad describes the role of a coach who develops and grows the individual into his or her desired maximum capacity and degree of accomplishment.

Islamic ideals echo in the authors' descriptive words for the stages of the coaching conversation: Discovery, Intentions, Pathways, Effort. Having discovered goals within him- or herself and examined the intentions behind them, the learner brainstorms paths to them that effort can enact. Probing the intentions of our acts and goals is already a move the Qur'an and Sunnah endorse. The very first Prophetic hadith in the canonical collection of *Sahih Bukhari* is "Actions are measured by intention", meaning that God determines the value of our actions by our intentions. The founder of the Shafi`i legal school of thought, Imam al-Shafi`i, famously said that in this one hadith is half of all wisdom.

For the benefit of Muslim readers, the authors have placed the value-free practice of coaching, as understood and applied in the West, within a framework of Islamic ethics. For, by way of an ingenious Alignment

Wheel unique to the Ershad method, Muslim coaches help their clients test their goals, and prospects for reaching them, against a framework of Muslim beliefs about God, self, others, and the world.

The joy the authors have experienced in their work communicates to us in their writing. If spirituality is itself a kind of alignment, of life with work, so that our work (whatever it may be) flows almost without our agency, then the authors themselves enact one vision of the spiritual life. The intent of the authors is for Ershad practices to guide others into that zone where God's work is present in ours, and God's pleasure in our acts. The line spoken by the champion runner in the movie *Chariots of Fire*, "When I run, I feel God's pleasure," clearly illustrates this desired state of action, a state sportspeople call being "in the zone". Psychologists have also called this a state of "flow".

That this occurred to the Prophet Muhammad is indicated by the occasion during the Battle of Badr, when he took a clump of dirt and threw it at his enemies. The Qur'an later revealed that "It was not you [O Prophet] who threw when you threw, but God who threw." Clearly, the Prophet Muhammad was then "in the zone".

The authors analogously want that we align our lives with the deepest goals we find in ourselves. For those are gifts from God which, when we find them, cause a switch to occur. At that point we no longer are the *rememberers* and God the *remembered*, but God becomes the rememberer and we the remembered. Now in the zone and in a state of flow, spirituality moves into high gear.

Islamic ethics flows out of that place of spiritual remembrance. And here again the authors practise what they preach. Their tone towards readers is warm and encouraging. They suggest that the skills of coaching—whether listening deeply to our partners in conversation, reflecting back to them what they have said to us, or prompting them with gentle questions to greater self-awareness—may already be functioning in our lives. They invite us, the readers, to heed the Delphic Oracle's dictum *to better know ourselves*, a dictum many Muslims attribute to the Prophet's cousin Imam Ali, and from which our spiritual masters have urged us for centuries, that *"He who knows his self, knows his Lord."* For the duration of the book the authors become our coaches, prompting us to excel at the work of betterment, both of ourselves and others.

We live in such noisy times. The noise is outside and within us. Amid the noise it is hard to hear what we, or anyone else, especially God, truly want for us. Listening is serious work. All coaching begins with deep listening, the authors tell us. Within a typical coaching conversation, a skilled coach speaks no more than twenty per cent of the time. The authors repeatedly underscore how important it is for the learner to feel heard. But this is true for all of us. If all of us are shouting, none of us is heard.

Not just coaches or would-be coaches will profit from this book. The advice of the authors, to listen empathically, speak non-judgementally, and transformatively guide the negative into the positive, applies to all of us. We can only share the authors' hope that the methods they outline for us will, as they say in their parting words, work to "build greater understanding between cultures" and more widely enjoyed betterment at "the policy and society level".

Imam Feisal Abdul Rauf
New York City, USA

INTRODUCTION

This book presents an approach to supporting people to achieve more of their potential. It is the result of a collaboration between two authors who share a passion and commitment for coaching which we define as the art and science of having conversations that encourage people to take responsibility for their own growth and development. Coaching is powerful because it is a way of supporting individuals to raise their self-awareness and take positive actions. Recipients of coaching often learn much about themselves. At the same time, coaching is also about encouraging people to be reflective, to take responsibility, and ultimately to do things differently. Our overriding aim is to enthuse readers and provide guidance about the appropriate use of coaching within Islamic culture.

Our intention

As we will discover together throughout this book, *intention* is a key factor in Islam and also in this approach to coaching. As a result, we must be clear about this at the outset. Our intention is to provide a culturally relevant coaching framework for use in Islamic contexts. We believe that coaching is a powerful conversational intervention that can support the growth and development of individuals. It can have transformational effects on individuals and significant impacts in organisational contexts.

More specifically, we intend to:

- Learn together
- Share our passion for coaching
- Explore effective coaching strategies
- Present a framework that allows Muslims to develop in ways that are aligned with their faith and traditions
- Propose a more balanced view of coaching in Islamic culture.

Learn together

The process of discussing, writing, and sharing our ideas has been a learning journey for both of us. We have benefited greatly from this process. It has developed our own understanding of coaching and an appreciation of how it can be used in various cultural contexts. We sincerely hope that you will join us on this journey of discovery as you read this book and start to practise Ershad coaching.

Share our passion for coaching

As authors, we have differing views, particular beliefs, and unique experiences of life, both personal and professional. However, we have worked together collaboratively on this project because we share a passion for coaching and its potential to make a positive difference in the lives of human beings. We have both experienced powerful coaching regarding our own development. And we are both executive coaches with many years of professional experience within the field. So from a personal perspective, we have benefited ourselves from coaching; and from a professional perspective we have seen the powerful impact that coaching can have on others. We hope to share our passion for coaching with you in the belief that this can support you in achieving what you need to achieve.

Explore effective coaching strategies

This book presents a complete coaching framework, which we call Ershad. We will share the key skills, the Ershad coaching process, the partnership conditions, and a necessary "way of being" that can lead to effective coaching practice. This is based on our own experience of delivering executive coaching and training others to become execu-tive coaches. We are building on evidence-based coaching models and approaches that have been used successfully for decades.

Present a framework that allows Muslims to develop in ways that are aligned with their faith and traditions

The clear and consistent driver for this book has been to present a *culturally appropriate* approach to coaching in Islamic culture. The idea for the book emerged when the authors met at a coaching conference in Kuwait in 2013. We felt that we wanted to explore the possibility of a culturally appropriate approach to coaching. After three years of talking, learning, and writing, we humbly propose that we have developed a framework that is more aligned with the faith and traditions of Muslims. We hope that you find this useful and would welcome your feedback.

Propose a more balanced view of coaching in Islamic culture

Although this was not a stated intention at the start of our collaboration, we hope that we can present a more balanced, positive view of Islam in this book. We are concerned about some inaccurate views about coach-ing in Islamic contexts. For example, Palmer and Arnold (2009) have highlighted the "impact of nepotism (wasta) on decision making" in the Arab world and propose that "Arabs like to talk more than work" (p. 113). While the conclusions are somewhat constructive ("We need to be aware of cultural differences", p. 114) such views reflect negative and unhelpful stereotypes which should have no place in coaching interac-tions. Such views only highlight the importance of mutually respectful interactions between cultures and people. Unfortunately, much of the writing about coaching in "other cultures" focuses on perceived *differences* between cultures, with Western culture invariably presented as an ideal. From this point of view, other cultures are seen as "developing", or inferior in some way.

"Ershad" coaching

We started writing this book with an open mind about the terminology that we would use. The options were:

- To use the existing English word: "coaching"
- To identify the new approach as "Islamic coaching"

- To adopt an Arabic word often used in this context: "tawjih"
- To explore different, more meaningful words during the writing process.

As an aside, the conference at which we met was called the "Kuwaiti Coaching Conference" which was translated as "Kuwaiti Conference for Tawjih". We agreed to start the project without committing to a particular title. From the outset, we were uncomfortable adopting the English word "coaching" for a number of reasons. First, even in the West, there is some confusion around the terminology. Second, we were keen to connect the coaching approach and framework to existing concepts within Islam. We were also concerned about the word "tawjih". In Arabic, this suggests showing someone the way or directing a person towards a solution. We felt that "tawjih" might be more appropriate as a translation for mentoring.

"Ershad" emerged gradually as our preferred term. The definition in the Arabic dictionary, *al-Maany al-Jami'*, includes concepts such as "guidance" and "enlightenment". It is used to refer to "being on the right path".

In adopting this word for our coaching framework, we want to highlight that we understand the Ershad coaching framework as a process of *self*-guidance. Essentially, it is the responsibility of the learner (coachee) to guide him- or herself towards the "right path" in the presence of a facilitator (coach) who manages the process. Together, the learner and facilitator work together to co-construct a safe, energising, and reflective space in which the self-guidance can take place. The Ershad coaching framework, therefore, allows the learner to set him- or herself on the right path according to his or her beliefs and values.

The Noble Qur'an

Obviously, we refer respectfully to the Noble Qur'an frequently in this textbook. After much consideration, we have chosen Arthur Arberry's English version, thoughtfully entitled *The Koran Interpreted* (1955). Arberry was a well-respected and highly regarded academic and scholar. He studied both Islam and Arabic and was a professor of Arabic at the University of Cambridge.

The use of "ar-rushd" (origin of ershad) occurs nineteen times within
the text of the Noble Qur'an in the following forms: ar-rushd, rashada,
ar-rushad, yarshudun, rashid, murshid, and al-rashidun. "Ra", "shin",
and "dal" are the three letters of the root word "ra-sha-da". When com-
bined, these three letters (ra-sha-da) signify the straight and narrow
path.

Below, we share some of the verses from the Noble Qur'an relating
to this concept:

لَا إِكْرَاهَ فِي الدِّينِ ۖ قَد تَّبَيَّنَ الرُّشْدُ مِنَ الْغَيِّ ۚ فَمَن يَكْفُرْ بِالطَّاغُوتِ وَيُؤْمِن بِاللهِ فَقَدِ اسْتَمْسَكَ بِالْعُرْوَةِ الْوُثْقَىٰ لَا انفِصَامَ لَهَا ۗ وَاللهُ سَمِيعٌ عَلِيمٌ - 2:256

2:256 No compulsion is there in religion. Rectitude [rushd] has become
clear from error. So whosoever disbelieves in idols and believes in God,
has laid hold of the most firm handle, unbreaking; God is All-hearing,
All-knowing.

إِذْ أَوَى الْفِتْيَةُ إِلَى الْكَهْفِ فَقَالُوا رَبَّنَا آتِنَا مِن لَّدُنكَ رَحْمَةً وَهَيِّئْ لَنَا مِنْ أَمْرِنَا رَشَدًا - 18:10

18:10 When the youths took refuge in the cave saying, "Our Lord, give us
mercy from Thee, and furnish us with rectitude [rashdan] in our affair."

إِلَّا أَن يَشَاءَ اللهُ ۚ وَاذْكُر رَّبَّكَ إِذَا نَسِيتَ وَقُلْ عَسَىٰ أَن يَهْدِيَنِ رَبِّي لِأَقْرَبَ مِنْ هَٰذَا رَشَدًا - 18:24

18:24 but only, "If God will"; and mention thy Lord, when thou for-
gettest, and say, "It may be that my Lord will guide me unto something
nearer to rectitude [rashadan] than this."

قَالَ لَهُ مُوسَىٰ هَلْ أَتَّبِعُكَ عَلَىٰ أَن تُعَلِّمَنِ مِمَّا عُلِّمْتَ رُشْدًا - 18:66

18:66 Moses said to him, "Shall I follow thee so that thou teachest me, of
what thou hast been taught, right judgment [rushdan]."

يَا قَوْمِ لَكُمُ الْمُلْكُ الْيَوْمَ ظَاهِرِينَ فِي الْأَرْضِ فَمَن يَنصُرُنَا مِن بَأْسِ اللهِ إِن جَاءَنَا ۚ قَالَ فِرْعَوْنُ مَا أُرِيكُمْ إِلَّا مَا أَرَىٰ وَمَا أَهْدِيكُمْ إِلَّا سَبِيلَ الرَّشَادِ - 40:29

40:29 "O my people, today the kingdom is yours, who are masters in the
land. But who will help us, against the might of God, if it comes upon

us?" Said Pharaoh, "I only let you see what I see; I only guide you in the way of rectitude [alrashadi]."

In the verses presented above, there is mention of being on the "right course", of receiving "right guidance", of undertaking "right conduct", and of learning "sound judgment". In this book, we present Ershad coaching as a methodology for supporting learners to identify the "right course" for themselves, supported by a facilitator. Ershad coaching, as we understand it, is a way of undertaking self-guidance, with the intention of enacting "right conduct" and adopting "sound judgment" in one's decisions.

Iqra

God revealed the Noble Qur'an to the Prophet Muhammad, peace be upon him, over a period of twenty-three years. While the Noble Qur'an has 114 chapters and over 6000 verses, the first word of the first verse revealed to the Prophet (96:1) is "Iqra". This word means to "read" and "recite". Teaching and learning are at the heart of Islam. We believe that the Ershad coaching framework can support individuals to learn, develop, and flourish.

In this book, we will use the word "coaching" to refer to the traditional practice of one-to-one conversations that focus on setting and achieving goals. Ershad coaching refers to the process of facilitated self-guidance through one-to-one conversations. As we will propose in this book, Ershad coaching includes three components: the partnership conditions, a conversational process, and an alignment wheel. So, Ershad coaching is a particular approach that supports learning, development, and flourishing that is aligned to one's values and beliefs. When referring to the practice of Ershad coaching, we will refer to a facilitator (the person who manages the conversational process) and a learner (the person who is undertaking self-guidance).

Outline of the book

Introduction

In the introduction, we have shared our intention as authors. We provide an explanation of why we have chosen the word "Ershad" and present a definition for its use in this context. There is also a brief outline of every chapter in order to give readers an overview of what is to follow.

Chapter One

Chapter One provides a brief overview of the historical context of coaching in Western culture. It explains the origins and current situation of the coaching profession. The differences between coaching and other one-to-one interventions are discussed.

Chapter Two

Chapter Two presents a review of the characteristics of Islamic culture that are relevant to the concept of coaching. There is also a brief exploration of guidance and mentoring in Islamic culture.

Chapter Three

The next three chapters explore the key skills of coaching. Chapter Three focuses on the important skill of listening. Specifically, readers will have an opportunity to reflect on the idea of "listening to understand rather than listening to solve". Some listening skills are presented.

Chapter Four

Chapter Four turns its attention to the skill of asking questions. In this chapter, readers are invited to think about ways of asking questions in order to provoke new thinking, rather than asking questions simply to get answers.

Chapter Five

Chapter Five covers two skills: summarising and paraphrasing. Both are important in coaching conversations. Readers will develop an understanding of the purpose of summarising with some strategies for doing this within coaching conversations. The role of paraphrasing within coaching conversations is also discussed.

Chapter Six

Chapter Six covers another two closely interrelated skills: giving and receiving feedback. We believe that facilitators of Ershad coaching should be good at giving feedback as well as receiving feedback. Some techniques for giving and receiving feedback are shared in this chapter.

Chapter Seven

Chapter Seven introduces the Ershad coaching framework. The chapter provides the rationale for the new framework before presenting it in detail. The "partnership conditions" are discussed and each phase of the conversational process is explained.

Chapter Eight

Chapter Eight provides information about an essential and integral part of the Ershad coaching framework: the "Alignment Wheel". The chapter discusses the concept of alignment in Islam. There is an explanation of three states of self that relate to Ershad coaching. This is followed by an exploration of the four relationships that can be discussed using the Alignment Wheel.

Chapter Nine

Chapter Nine presents the concept of a "coaching way of being" (van Nieuwerburgh, 2017). This is based on the idea that the way of being of the facilitator is an important factor in the outcome of Ershad coaching relationships. It is argued that the facilitator and the learner should work in close partnership. There is a discussion about the connection between faith, balance, and well-being.

Chapter Ten

Chapter Ten brings the book to a conclusion. We highlight the importance of "starting with oneself". We share some information about the way that we worked together (as authors) and conclude with some comments about the global application of the Ershad coaching framework.

Chapter Eleven

This chapter presents a number of case studies. Each discusses a particular experience of coaching within an Islamic context.

Ongoing journey

We hope that you will find this to be an enjoyable and fruitful journey of learning. We certainly have! Learning to become a facilitator of Ershad coaching will provide you with many transferable skills. We also believe that you will learn much about yourself and find ways to improve outcomes and relationships in your own life. As the authors, we are learning all the time, and welcome the opportunity to learn from you. Please feel free to get in touch with us with your comments, ideas, and feedback.

CHAPTER ONE

A brief history of coaching

A t the start of this book, we think it would be helpful to survey the history of coaching in order to gain a better understanding of its origins. While executive coaching has been flourishing as an optimal way of enhancing performance since the early 1990s, the concept of a supportive relationship based on meaningful conversations has a long history.

Ancient Greece

The very first reference to this kind of supportive relationship occurs in a Greek myth as told in Homer's *The Odyssey*. In this tale, Odysseus's son, Telemachus, is supported by a wise old man called "Mentor". Subsequently, the word "mentor" has become associated with the figure of a wise and trusted adviser based on this literary character. Historically, the Ancient Greeks provided dedicated support for their elite athletes. The most promising athletes would practise in gymnasia, supported by former champions of the same sport. It should be noted that they did not use the term "coach" for this role. However, although they used the word "gymnastes" to describe these former champions, this equates broadly to the role of the modern sports coach.

1

The Hungarian town

The word "coach" is thought to have originated from the name of a town in Hungary (Koc, pronounced "kotch") that used to build carriages in the fifteenth century. The type of light, fast carriage they built became popular across Europe. The English word "coach" is thought to derive from the Hungarian word "kocsi" which means "from the town of Koc". It is believed that coaches (and the word "coach") came into use in England in the sixteenth century.

University of Oxford

The first usage of the word "coach" to refer to a *person* seems to be in an academic context, at the University of Oxford in the 1830s (*Online Etymology Dictionary*). In this case, the word "coach" was used to refer to a tutor who supported a student with his or her academic work. It is believed that it was initially used informally, implying that a tutor would take a student from point A (not knowing what he or she needed to know in order to pass an examination) to point B (having good knowledge of the material in order to pass an examination)—much like a coach (or carriage) which would also take people from point A to point B.

Sports coaching

Coaching has been central to elite sporting performance for generations. The year 1861 is the first time the word "coaching" can be identified as being used in an athletic sense. From the 1860s onwards, coaching has been used in the sports context in England, with sports coaches supporting athletes to excel in their chosen fields. Sports coaching has developed quickly and significantly into a professional field (Day & Carpenter, 2016). Nowadays almost every sports team has a coach—and every elite athlete is supported to achieve greatness by a dedicated coach.

Business

The business world has always been interested in the possibility of improving human performance. At times in its history, it has been particularly attracted to exploring how to improve human performance through psychology. Between the 1940s and 1960s, some organisations provided their senior executives with counselling, delivered by occupational or organisational psychologists. These interventions were designed to support the executives to overcome barriers and excel at their work.

Humanistic psychology

The modern incarnation of coaching can trace its roots back to the Human Potential Movement of the 1960s, a decade of exploration in human growth and development. Two eminent psychologists, Abraham Maslow and Carl Rogers, were champions of human potential and leading figures in the field of humanistic psychology. This movement promoted an optimistic view of human nature, arguing that people had an urge to achieve their full potential. As a result, the movement advised employers of the importance of treating their people well, rather than focusing entirely on performance improvements.

Inner game

The concept of the "inner game" was proposed by Tim Gallwey in his 1974 book, *The Inner Game of Tennis*. In this revolutionary text, Gallwey suggested that the "inner game" of a player (psychological attitude) was as important as the "external game" (physical skill and competencies). In other words, the struggle against one's own doubts, fears, and self-limiting beliefs was as important as the struggle against an external opponent. Although this first book addressed the question of the "inner game" of a tennis player, it soon became apparent that the concept could apply to any situation. This theory was embraced by the business community in the US in the 1970s and 1980s. It was brought to the UK by Graham Alexander and John Whitmore who had learned the approach from Gallwey when they were in the US. Linking up with a global consultancy firm, Alexander and Whitmore developed the concept into the well-known GROW model that is now taught in most coach training programmes. Following the publication of Whitmore's book *Coaching for Performance* in 1992, executive coaching started to flourish in the UK in the final years of the twentieth century and has been gaining momentum steadily since then. Coaching is currently being used to support students, business leaders, patients, health professionals, future leaders, senior executives—in fact anyone who wishes to achieve more of their potential.

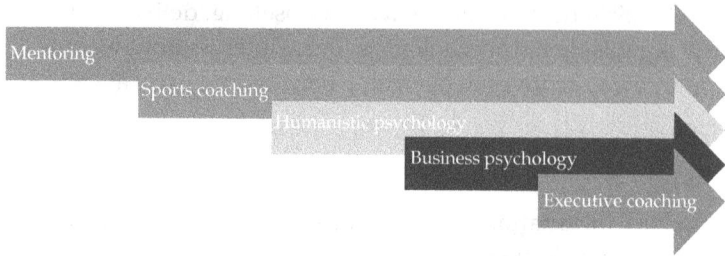

Figure 1.1. The sources of executive coaching.

Today: professional contexts

Executive coaching is today firmly embedded in many Western cultures. It is often used in educational settings (van Nieuwerburgh, 2012) and is popular across a wide range of professional contexts (van Nieuwerburgh, 2016). Executive coaching has come to be viewed as an individualised form of personal and professional development. While generic skills can still be taught through traditional training days, it is now believed that more sophisticated professional development for leaders and executives can be delivered through one-to-one coaching. It is seen as timely, on-the-job professional development. One-to-one coaching arrangements for senior leaders, coaching to support and embed professional development, and access to coaching across organisations are now commonplace.

The last two decades have witnessed an explosion of interest, with many hundreds of training organisations delivering coach training programmes. These range from one-day short courses, online courses, week-long certificated programmes to postgraduate level qualifications. Coaching is in use in professional contexts in many of the world's leading economies (Ridler Report, 2016; Sherpa Executive Coaching Survey, 2015). Furthermore, coaching is now a profession in its own right with a number of professional associations (e.g., International Coaching Federation; Association for Coaching; European Mentoring and Coaching Council; Association for Professional Executive Coaching and Supervision).

Today: the academic field

The academic underpinnings and evidence base for coaching initially came from a number of different fields, including sports, counselling, education, psychotherapy, and psychology. More recently, there is research and study on coaching directly through two emergent academic fields: coaching psychology and positive psychology. It is possible to undertake a postgraduate qualification such as MA or MSc in coaching. The earliest of these programmes were launched in Australia and the United Kingdom in the 1990s. Such programmes are now delivered in British universities within psychology, education, and business departments and an increasing number of universities globally.

A mark of the recognition of the business and leadership potential of executive coaching is the fact that some of the world's elite business schools now deliver postgraduate courses in executive coaching. Henley Business School and INSEAD, for example, both deliver such programmes.

The field of coaching now has its own academic, peer-reviewed journals, including *Coaching: An International Journal of Theory, Research and Practice, The International Journal of Evidence-based Coaching and Mentoring*, and the *International Coaching Psychology Review*. There are special interest groups dedicated to coaching within the American Psychological Association (APA), the Australian Psychological Society (APS), and the British Psychological Society (BPS).

Research into coaching

Since the 1990s, there have been concerted efforts within the field to broaden the evidence base of coaching in the academic arena (Passmore & Fillery-Travis, 2011). Early qualitative studies and case studies have been followed more recently by small-scale quantitative and mixed methods studies (Passmore & Theeboom, 2015). Broadly speaking, it has been possible to demonstrate that coaching is having positive effects on performance, well-being, goal attainment, and attitudes to work (Theeboom, 2016). While the academic field is still in its infancy compared to more established areas of study, the initial findings are encouraging and bode well for the future of coaching.

Defining the term

The rapid development of the profession of coaching has also had some shortcomings. One of these is the lack of definitional clarity of the term "coaching". This is due, in part, to the mixed heritage of coaching.

Having emerged from mentoring, sports coaching, and the humanistic tradition, executive coaching is seen in a number of different ways by professionals. The commercial drivers to present coaching as "all things to all people" has also played a part in muddying the waters. Below, we will outline our definition of executive coaching so that we can bring some clarity to our own discussion in this book.

Well-known definitions

Perhaps the best-known coaching definition is that proposed by Sir John Whitmore:

> "Unlocking people's potential to maximise their own performance.
> It is helping them to learn rather than teaching them" (2009, p. 11).

Below are a few other definitions that provide a few slightly different views about coaching:

- "The art of facilitating the unleashing of people's potential to reach meaningful, important objectives" (Rosinski, 2003, p. 4)
- "The art of facilitating the performance, learning and development of another" (Downey, 2003, p. 21)
- "Coaching is a method of work-related learning that relies primarily on one-to-one conversations" (de Haan, 2008, p. 19)
- "Coaching is a human development process that involves structured, focused interaction and the use of appropriate strategies, tools and techniques to promote desirable and sustainable change for the benefit of the coachee and potentially for other stakeholders" (Bachkirova, Cox, & Clutterbuck, 2014, p. 1)
- "Executive coaching is a conversational process that leads to a change in thinking or behaviour with the aim of improving outcomes in professional contexts" (van Nieuwerburgh, 2016, p. 3).

Broadly speaking, there is agreement that coaching:

1. Is a managed conversation that takes place between two people
2. Aims to support sustainable change to behaviours or ways of thinking
3. Focuses on learning and development (van Nieuwerburgh, 2017, p. 5).

Coaching and mentoring

Coaching and mentoring are closely related terms as we have discussed earlier. Coaches and mentors share similar skills and processes. Mentors, however, are expected to have expert information about the topic of discussion. Mentoring is a process for transferring knowledge, insights, and expertise from one person to another. Coaches, on the other hand, do not need to have expert knowledge about the topic being discussed. The role of the coach is to support a coachee to generate his or her own solutions and ideas. The mentor can be seen as an adviser or wise counsellor while the coach is more of a facilitator and thinking partner.

A key differentiator is the directivity or non-directivity of the person in the supporting role. Although both coaches and mentors can direct the conversational process, the coach is non-directive when it comes to what the coachee should do. This means that the coach does not advise, guide, or make suggestions about actions that a coachee might undertake. On the other hand, the mentor has a more directive role. Mentors are expected to provide suggestions, share insights, and impart guidance. As you can see, both roles have the same intention of supporting the coachee or mentee. In coaching, the support takes the form of facilitation while in mentoring, the support involves direct guidance.

Coaching and counselling

Coaching and counselling also share many similarities. In both cases, one person (the coach or counsellor) listens empathetically to the client as they work through the topic that the client has brought to the session. Both are one-to-one, confidential, and meaningful conversations. The coach's role is to support the coachee to identify a desired future state or goal and then listen and ask questions as the coachee explores ways of moving forward. A counsellor is more likely to be needed when the client requires support to resolve complex psychological issues that have occurred in the past.

A key differentiator between coaching and counselling, therefore, is whether the conversation is focused on the past or on the future. It has been proposed that coaching should focus on the present and the future, while counselling tends to focus on uncovering and resolving problematic issues from a person's past.

Coaching and consultancy

Coaching and consultancy are also closely aligned activities. Effective coaching and consultancy should start from building an understanding of the client's current situation. Both approaches should be working to help the clients to generate relevant, tailor-made solutions. However, consultants are employed in order to provide solutions for their clients. Often, they are expected to be experts in their clients' professional context. Coaches, on the other hand, are employed to support their clients to think through challenges for themselves. For a coach, having experience of the client's professional context may be helpful for credibility but this is not essential.

Our experience

As authors, we have significant experience of executive coaching. We are both qualified executive coaches with experience of coaching clients in the Middle East, the United States, Europe, and Australia. We also spend a significant amount of our time training others to become coaches. One of us has experience of teaching on postgraduate coach training programmes at British universities while the other delivers accredited coaching courses in the Gulf region. In this book, we have brought together our shared experiences, learning, and research about a topic that we are both passionate about. This writing project is part of our ongoing learning process.

Conclusion

In this chapter, we have provided a brief overview of the history of coaching. We discussed the current popularity of coaching and its growth commercially and academically. We have concluded by defining the term "coaching" and differentiating it from other related conversational interventions. In the next chapter, we will consider coaching and guidance from an Islamic perspective.

CHAPTER TWO

Coaching in Islamic culture

Having considered the history and development of coaching in the West in the previous chapter, we will now turn our attention to the Islamic context. Our intention in this chapter is to consider the applicability of coaching within Islamic culture. Rather than attempt a review of Islamic culture in general, we have instead focused on the context for coaching, with particular interest in the relevant characteristics of Islamic culture.

The concept of Islamic culture

In this chapter we will be discussing the practical knowledge and traditions derived from Islam that affect conscious human behaviour and society. We shall call this "Islamic culture". The legitimate sources of Islamic culture are the Noble Qur'an, the Sunnah, and the consensus of Muslim scholars based on a body of knowledge including Islamic history, Arabic language, and human experience. We propose that knowledge and understanding of Islamic culture is necessary for coaches working in such contexts. The characteristics below are based on the work of Al Marsafi (2008).

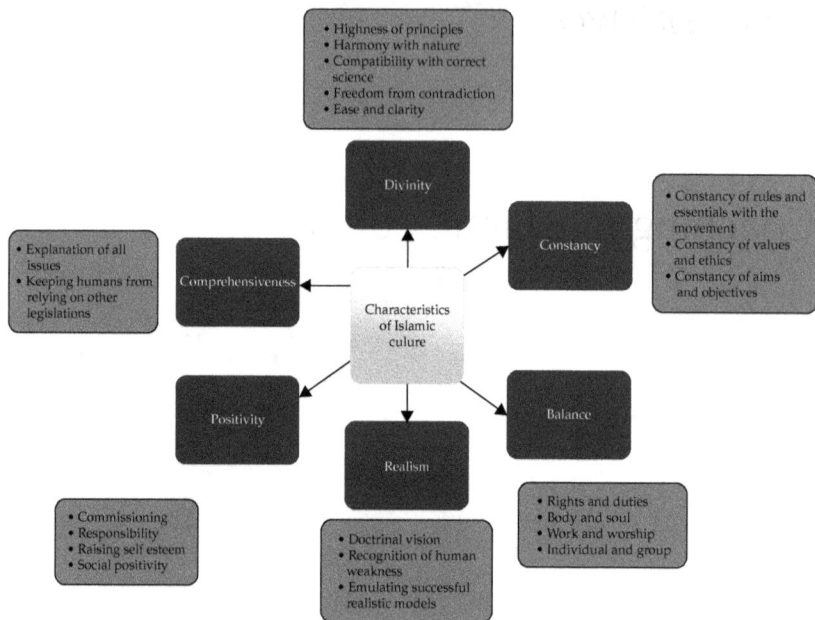

Figure 2.1. The key characteristics of Islamic culture.

Characteristics of Islamic culture

Divinity

The first and most important characteristic of Islamic culture is that it originates from a divine source. In the words of God: "… then they would not be respited. It is We who have sent down the Remembrance [the Noble Qu'ran], and We watch over it" (15:9). Therefore, we can conclude that the conception and existence of Islamic culture, with all its characteristics and components, is derived from God.

إِنَّا نَحْنُ نَزَّلْنَا الذِّكْرَ وَإِنَّا لَهُ لَحَافِظُونَ - 15:9

Implications of the divinity of Islamic culture

1. The principles, values, and validity of this culture are divine.
2. As such, Islamic culture is compatible with human nature and a healthy mind.

3. Islamic culture should therefore be free of contradiction and conflict.
4. Islamic culture brings pleasure and clear thinking to human beings.

Constancy

Islamic culture is characterised by the absolute constancy of its rules, references, sources, and values. According to God: "Then We set thee [O Muhammad] upon an open way of the Command; therefore follow it, and follow not the caprices of those who do not know" (45:18).

ثُمَّ جَعَلْنَاكَ عَلَىٰ شَرِيعَةٍ مِّنَ الْأَمْرِ فَاتَّبِعْهَا وَلَا تَتَّبِعْ أَهْوَاءَ الَّذِينَ لَا يَعْلَمُونَ - 45:18

Furthermore, "And that this is My path, straight; so do you follow it, and follow not divers[e] paths lest they scatter you from His path. That then He has charged you with; haply you will be godfearing" (6:153).

وَأَنَّ هَٰذَا صِرَاطِي مُسْتَقِيمًا فَاتَّبِعُوهُ ۖ وَلَا تَتَّبِعُوا السُّبُلَ فَتَفَرَّقَ بِكُمْ عَن سَبِيلِهِ ۚ ذَٰلِكُمْ وَصَّاكُم بِهِ لَعَلَّكُمْ تَتَّقُونَ - 6:153

We should note, however, that constancy should not be understood as causing stagnation or stifling human creativity and activity. On the contrary, this constancy is understood to encourage human endeavour, creativity, and development within the framework of Islamic culture.

Implications of the constancy of Islamic culture

1. Islamic culture requires human beings to adjust their activity and endeavours to meet the expectations of a specific framework. This is so that people do not deviate from the righteous path.
2. Islamic culture requires human beings to adjust their thoughts so as not to be torn with desires, passions, and unhelpful influences. Muslims need not be affected by the words of others whether they are close or distant, senior or subordinate, powerful or powerless.
3. Islamic culture provides the Muslim community with the strong protection of ideological beliefs.
4. Islamic culture guarantees constancy in standards used to measure the work of all people. In Islam, there should be no favouritism nor differentiation. Persons—great or humble—are equal before Islamic principles and in Islamic society. In confirmation of this sense,

the Messenger of God said: "What was withering for those before you, that if among them a powerful one steals they let him go and if a powerless one steals they punish him. I swear to God, if Fatima daughter of Muhammad would have stolen, I would cut off her hand" (Bukhari 4:681).

5. Islamic culture allows for the retention of the identity, character, and existence of the Islamic nation so it cannot dissolve amid other cultures and civilisations.

Comprehensiveness

Islamic culture deals with all aspects of worship, relationships, sociology, economy, management, justice, administration, and foreign policy. It covers all fields of life. Islamic culture considers all human beings in their different stages of life, across multiple relationships, and their spiritual and material needs. God says in the Noble Qur'an: "And We have sent down on thee the Book making clear everything, and as a guidance and a mercy, and as good tidings to those who surrender" (16:89).

وَنَزَّلْنَا عَلَيْكَ الْكِتَابَ تِبْيَانًا لِّكُلِّ شَيْءٍ وَهُدًى وَرَحْمَةً وَبُشْرَىٰ لِلْمُسْلِمِينَ - 16:89

It is a culture that reflects its comprehensiveness in all its dealings with humans, the universe, and life.

Implications of the comprehensiveness of Islamic culture

1. Islamic culture provides an explanation of major issues that occupy human thought so that people can feel tranquility through knowledge of their origin and upbringing. They can understand their fate and their end, their relationship with God and their own role in this existence. Through this knowledge, human beings can find a safe haven to enjoy tranquility and stability in their lives.
2. Islam provides the necessary legislation and regulation that people require in their private and public lives.

Positivity

Islamic culture is characterised as a positive culture. It calls for humans to undertake work that is in line with each person's capacity, potential, and talent. This culture strongly warns against dependence, cowardice, and laziness: "God changes not what is in a people, until they change what is in themselves" (13:11).

إِنَّ اللَّهَ لَا يُغَيِّرُ مَا بِقَوْمٍ حَتَّىٰ يُغَيِّرُوا مَا بِأَنفُسِهِمْ ۗ - 13:11

Islamic culture does not allow Muslims to be disengaged, living on the margins of life without affecting the surrounding universe and environment. It celebrates Muslims who are positive about their faith and care about other Muslims and their affairs. God praised the Islamic nation for demonstrating its positivity: "You are the best nation ever brought forth to men" (3:110).

كُنتُمْ خَيْرَ أُمَّةٍ أُخْرِجَتْ لِلنَّاسِ تَأْمُرُونَ بِالْمَعْرُوفِ وَتَنْهَوْنَ عَنِ الْمُنكَرِ وَتُؤْمِنُونَ بِاللَّهِ ۗ وَلَوْ آمَنَ أَهْلُ الْكِتَابِ
لَكَانَ خَيْرًا لَّهُم ۚ مِّنْهُمُ الْمُؤْمِنُونَ وَأَكْثَرُهُمُ الْفَاسِقُونَ - 3:110

Implications of the positivity of Islamic culture

1. Islamic culture supports Muslims to feel that they should do their best because they have been provided with the preparation, talents, and potential needed. They can be confident that God will help them carry out their work diligently, guiding their footsteps and supporting them.
2. Islamic culture allows Muslims to understand the greatness of their responsibility and their importance in life. Muslims will understand that they were not created in vain, but through God's wisdom and good fortune. By taking positive action, they fulfil the will of God, and their existence on earth requires continuous work, both on their own and with others around them.
3. Islamic culture elevates Muslims, raising their value in their own and others' eyes, escalating their interests, aims, and objectives. Muslims should not compete with people on trivial issues or personal interests.
4. Islamic culture promotes social positivity through a requirement to pay attention to brothers and sisters, and to share with them, whether they are relatives, neighbours, acquaintances, or friends.

Realism

Islamic culture is characterised by the great advantage of realism. Islam is realistic because it is based on the faith of divine truth and demonstrations of the effects of God's power: "So glory be to God both in your evening hour and in your morning hour. His is the praise in the heavens and earth, alike at the setting sun and in your noontide hour. He brings forth the living from the dead, and brings forth the dead from the living, and He revives the earth after it is dead; even so you shall be brought forth" (30:17–19).

فَسُبْحَانَ اللَّهِ حِينَ تُمْسُونَ وَحِينَتُصْبِحُونَ - 30:17 وَلَهُ الْحَمْدُ فِي السَّمَاوَاتِ وَالْأَرْضِ وَعَشِيًّا وَحِينَ تُظْهِرُونَ - 30:18 يُخْرِجُ الْحَيَّ مِنَ الْمَيِّتِ وَيُخْرِجُ الْمَيِّتَ مِنَ الْحَيِّ وَيُحْيِي الْأَرْضَ بَعْدَ مَوْتِهَا ۚ وَكَذَٰلِكَ تُخْرَجُونَ - 30:19

Islam is based on realism because it offers a practical and comprehensive approach for life on earth. It deals with each person based on his or her reality: "God charges no soul save to its capacity" (2:286).

لَا يُكَلِّفُ اللَّهُ نَفْسًا إِلَّا وُسْعَهَا ۚ - 2:286

Implications of the realism of Islamic culture

1. Muslims should undertake their religious duties with energy because such duties are based on their capabilities, capacities, and limitations.
2. Islamic culture recognises human weakness. It does not deal with Muslims as angels, but as human beings. In other words, Muslims do wrong and right and learn from their mistakes. However, Islam calls upon Muslims not to accept errors and be satisfied with them.
3. Muslims are called upon to challenge weakness and whim with determination to succeed.
4. Muslims can emulate others who have practised Islam in their lives. Therefore, they have practical examples to follow.

Balance

The word "balance" in Arabic is derived from the scales (i.e., even distribution of weight, which includes a sense of consistency, harmony, interdependence, and communication). Such a sense of balance is established in the Noble Qur'an in which God says: "And heaven—He raised it up, and set the Balance. (Transgress not in the Balance, and weigh with justice, and skimp not in the Balance)" (55:7–9).

وَالسَّمَاءَ رَفَعَهَا وَوَضَعَ الْمِيزَانَ - 55:7 أَلَّا تَطْغَوْا فِي الْمِيزَانِ - 55:8 وَأَقِيمُوا الْوَزْنَ بِالْقِسْطِ وَلَا تُخْسِرُوا الْمِيزَانَ - 55:9

In Islamic culture, there is a balance between rights and duties; among rights with each other and among duties with each other; and a balance between the demands of the soul and those of the body. Muslims are required to worship God but are commanded to spend some attention on themselves, their children, and their community. People are ordered to be concerned with the hereafter, but not to forget their share of life in this world. God says: "… but seek, amidst that which God has given thee, the Last Abode, and forget not thy portion of the present world; and do good, as God has been good to thee. And seek not to work corruption in the earth; surely God loves not the workers of corruption" (28:77).

وَابْتَغِ فِيمَا آتَاكَ اللهُ الدَّارَ الْآخِرَةَ وَلَا تَنسَ نَصِيبَكَ مِنَ الدُّنْيَا وَأَحْسِن كَمَا أَحْسَنَ اللهُ إِلَيْكَ وَلَا تَبْغِ الْفَسَادَ فِي الْأَرْضِ إِنَّ اللهَ لَا يُحِبُّ الْمُفْسِدِينَ - 28:77

Implications of the balance of Islamic culture

1. Muslims should be aware of the balance between the unseen world which the mind cannot realise, and the seen world, which the mind can perceive.
2. Muslims should be aware of the balance between human effectiveness in the universe and the relationship of the universe to human beings.
3. Muslims should be aware of the balance between worship and work. Worship rituals and practical activities both have their time and place.
4. Muslims should be aware of the balance between individuals and the group, so that individuals do not contravene the group's rights, and the group should not harm the rights of individuals.

In the section above, we have reviewed some of the key characteristics of Islamic culture, highlighting the implications that may be relevant to coaching. Below, we will provide a brief overview of the role that guidance and mentoring have had in Islamic culture.

Guidance and mentoring in Islam

Guidance plays an important part in Islamic culture. According to Abu Ghazaleh, "Guidance is the key mechanism in mentoring and supporting operations, forming the centre of the interactive relationship that develops between the educational guide and his or her audience. Guidance can be provided through different methods, directly or indirectly, individually or collectively. It can also adopt various approaches such as observation, discussion, decision-making, and choices" (1978, p. 133). At its core is the relationship between the guide and the learner and its purpose is to provide support with learning and development. Abu Ghazaleh proposes that "Guidance may be used for professional, educational, or psychological counselling and for other similar purposes" (1978, p. 133). This definition is echoed by Zahran who describes guidance as "a constructive process that aims to help the individual to understand themselves, studying their character to identify problems but also to develop their potential as a key solution, tapping into their knowledge, education, and training as well as their own desires and motivations to achieve mental health and compatibility, as a person, in their schools, jobs, or families" (1980, p. 11). It becomes evident from these definitions that guidance is suitable for a wide range of applications, from psychological to educational to professional. It can incorporate self-awareness as well as external knowledge and understanding. According to Omar, guidance can also be a way of dealing with a person's "personal problems" in order to "take charge and make decisions to solve their problems objectively" (1984, p. 40), and Al-Khatib proposes that guidance is "a human relationship between a trained specialist and a person seeking assistance" (2004, p. 72). In Islamic culture, the goals of guidance are to:

- Address the problems of individuals and society
- Achieve a balance in human relationships
- Achieve well-being in this world and the hereafter
- Learn about Islam itself
- Encourage self-discipline
- Strengthen faith in God (Abdelrahman al Isawi, 1992)

Al-Hayani (1989), al-Mighmasy (1993) and Mahmoud (1998) all propose that guidance can help individuals to solve a wide range of issues, from the spiritual to the social to the academic. In 1997, al-Sayyid argued that these types of conversations should take place "within a moderate Islamic framework" (p. 26).

The general trend of thinking is bringing the concept of guidance closer to the way that coaching has been used in the West over the last few decades. For example, according to Al-Ani, guidance is considered to be a "structured and planned, human process" (2000, p. 60). More recent writers have defined guidance as a methodology for helping "the individual understand themselves and identify their potential, their own abilities and skills" (Abbas & Mohammed, 2009, p. 24). The overlap between this way of describing guidance and existing definitions of coaching (surveyed in Chapter One) is significant.

Up to this point, writers have been using the words "guidance" and "mentoring" interchangeably to refer to conversational practices that span a wide range of aspects, from psychological to social, educational to spiritual, and personal to professional. This lack of clarity regarding definitions and the scope of a professional's work may be interfering with the development of positive approaches for use in guidance, mentoring, and coaching. In this book, our intention is to provide some clear distinctions, presenting an integrated framework for coaching to support people to pursue their positive intentions and aspirations. We believe that coaching should focus on proactive clients who are seeking better results and greater alignment in their lives.

To provide some further clarity, it is helpful to outline and distinguish between the roles of professionals who can support the learning and development of others in Islamic culture. Below we present a table that shows the similarities and differences in the roles of preachers, teachers, and coaches. In the table, we are identifying skills and competencies that we believe are *essential* for each of the roles. This is not to imply that some of these professionals may not have a broader range of skills and competencies.

Teacher: preacher: coach

The teacher

The role of a teacher is to help other people to learn new information and gain knowledge. A teacher requires specific subject knowledge and well-developed pedagogical skills. He or she works tirelessly to create challenging, nurturing environments for learners. Teachers

Table 2.1. Differences between teachers, preachers, and coaches.

	Teacher	Preacher	Coach
Knowledge			
Expertise in the relevant field	x	x	
Ability to give informed advice and guidance	x	x	
Detailed, scholarly and technical knowledge of Islam		x	
Ability to promote that which is good and talk about Islamic faith	x	x	x
Meaningful religious belief	x	x	x
Competency			
Ethics and integrity	x	x	x
Having presence	x	x	x
Skills			
Building trust	x	x	x
Ability to use a coaching framework			x
Active listening			x
Powerful questioning			x
Managing one-to-one relationships			x
Giving and receiving feedback	x		x
Ability to challenge others in a supportive way	x		x

require the following attributes or skills in order to fulfil their role in Islamic culture:

1. Scientific competency: the ability to provide the knowledge and experiences needed by students of the topic.
2. Educational competency: the knowledge of appropriate educational methods in order to deliver engaging learning experiences.
3. Communication competency: the ability to communicate with students in order to engage them and disseminate information, ideas, and skills.
4. Desire or passion: a deeply held belief in the value of education and a desire to support others to learn and develop.

In addition to the above, teachers will be effective if they are empathetic and courageous with a strong set of values.

(Adapted from GEMS Learning Gateway)

The preacher

The preacher is a person who has a deep knowledge of Islam. This knowledge should be at technical, scholarly, and practical levels. Preachers are able to speak confidently about Islamic beliefs, theology, jurisprudence, and morals. The Noble Qur'an calls on all believers to promote what is good and to forbid that which is not. Preachers require God to fulfil their missions and need the following attributes or skills in order to discharge their roles in Islamic culture:

1. Accurate and detailed understanding based on scholarship, and an ability to contemplate the meanings and insights of the Noble Qur'an, the Sunnah, and the prophetic tradition.
2. Deep, meaningful faith and a love of God, a fear of God, hope in God's blessing, and the ability to follow His messengers and all of their messages.
3. A connection to God in all of their work as well as sole dedication to Him in their words and actions.

In addition to the above, preachers require deeply held ethics and values. They are required to be good examples to others.

The coach

A coach is a person who supports others to grow and develop towards their desired futures. Coaches should be skilled at managing conversations and possess knowledge of tools and techniques for supporting sustainable change in others. It has been proposed that there are three elements to effective coaching: a conversational process; a set of communication skills; and a particular "coaching way of being" (van Nieuwerburgh, 2017). Therefore, coaches require the following attributes or skills in order to fulfil their roles in Islamic culture:

1. Faith: A good coach should have faith. His or her approach should be informed by the teachings of the Noble Qur'an, the Sunnah, and prophetic tradition.

2. Modelling: it is important that coaches should be able to "walk the talk". As he or she is interested in the success and well-being of their coachees in this life and the hereafter, the coach should act as a role model for a good way of living.
3. Initiative: the coach should have a desire to undertake this important, humanitarian work. Coaches should develop their understanding of people and be prepared to study the skills, process, and way of being required for effective coaching.
4. Discretion: coaches must be able to maintain confidentiality. Whatever is discussed during a coaching conversation should not be revealed by a coach.
5. Positive thinking: the coach should think well of his or her coachees. What coachees say should be interpreted positively, assuming that it is spoken with good intentions.

In addition to the above, coaches should be committed to continual self-development and learning through reflective practice.

Conclusion

In this chapter, we have provided some contextual information for the use of coaching within Islamic culture. We have presented some relevant characteristics of Islamic culture, reflecting on how each of these may impact on the practice of coaching. There has been a short survey of guidance and mentoring within Islamic culture. We have also provided a working definition of coaching. The practice of coaching is compared with the related activities of teaching and preaching.

Ultimately, we have identified that personal support for development can be an essential part of Islamic culture. We are proposing that coaching can play an important role in supporting the growth, development, and success of Muslims. In the next chapters, we will consider some of the key skills required by coaches.

CHAPTER THREE

Listening with purpose

Power of listening

Senior managers, chief executives, students, doctors, educators, and professionals from a wide variety of fields report that coaching has resulted in significant and sustained positive changes in their lives. This has been experienced by both of the authors of this book. Our lives have been altered, influenced, and enhanced as a result of our own experiences of being coached. The reality is that life-changing insights, new ideas, and profound realisations can emerge from thought-provoking conversations between two individuals. We all recognise this. But how is this possible? And what actually takes place within these conversations? And finally, what is the role of a coach in this type of transformational conversation?

Let us start our exploration of these questions by focusing firstly on the most important of the skills of a coach: the ability to listen fully to the coachee. Before anything else, the coach must adopt the role of an interested listener. In fact, observation of coaching practice suggests that the most effective conversations are those in which the coach spends the most time listening. Often, the coach is silent for about 80–90 per cent of the coaching session. To put it bluntly, the best coaches do very little talking. From this perspective, it may seem that coaching could be a very unbalanced conversation (compared to traditional social interactions). However, this is appropriate in these situations because the purpose of coaching is to support the coachee to speak about and think through what is on his or her mind. In other words, we *do* want the coachee to feel that the conversation is one-sided. It is his or her opportunity to be listened to. In this case, the coachee is the "lead thinker and learner".

If the coachee is the lead thinker and learner, then the coach has a secondary, but vital role. The coach's role is to create the best possible environment in which the coachee can think clearly. The purpose of this environment is to allow the coachee to reflect in order to develop new perspectives and insights. It has been argued convincingly that the quality of a coach's listening has a direct relationship to the quality of a coachee's thinking (Kline, 1999). So the two roles must work together to ensure the best chance of success. (This partnership will be discussed in more detail in Chapter Seven.)

In your experience

You may have had an experience that may help to elucidate this point. Have you ever been speaking to someone about a topic that is of interest to you, and then noticed that they are distracted and not listening? In this case, it is normal for you to lose track of what you have been trying to say. Sometimes, faced with a person who is obviously not interested in our ideas, we can start to get confused or lose our words. This is an example of the negative aspect of the concept we are discussing here. However, the opposite seems to have a positive effect. Listening with interest and enthusiasm can help the speaker to be more coherent, increasing in confidence about the topic, thus supporting him or her to improve the quality of his or her thinking.

If we accept that effective coaches devote up to 80 or 90 per cent of their professional time listening, it is logical to think that they should have highly developed listening skills. Below, we shall consider the idea of "listening with purpose".

Listening with purpose

Obviously, as members of families, educational institutions, and society, most of us have developed the ability to listen to others.

For the majority of people, this experience relates to day-to-day conversational listening. In such conversations, we tend to say something, stop while our partners respond (during which time we listen to what they have to say), and then, in turn, we reply to their comment. This way of interacting requires us to listen to the input coming to us from our conversational partner *and* also think about how we will respond to the point that we are hearing. This forces us to take some attention away from listening to the other person and start to formulate our responses in order to avoid any awkward silences in the conversation.

While this kind of listening is a helpful and necessary conversational skill, coaches are required to develop a different way of listening. For coaches to be successful, they should be able to listen to their coachees in a way that:

- Increases the self-awareness of the coachee
- Values the coachee
- Shows interest in the topic being discussed
- Creates "thinking space"
- Builds trust.

Increasing the self-awareness of the coachee

One of the starting points for a person to begin to make plans for sustainable changes in the future is a good understanding of his or her current situation. This means that a coach should have the skill to listen attentively while the coachee tries to make sense of what is happening in his or her professional or personal life. Sometimes, simply explaining the current reality to a coach can lead to an increased understanding of that situation. The very act of verbalising one's thoughts can lead to new perspectives or clearer insights.

For example

One coachee was discussing his dissatisfaction with his current job. The coach simply asked the coachee to tell him about what led to the feelings of dissatisfaction. Below is a transcript from the coaching conversation.

Coach: So what has led to this dissatisfaction?
Coachee: So many things ...

Coach:	[Remains silent]
Coachee:	So many things. I really don't know where to start. Money. But also promotion. I mean, lack of promotion.
Coach:	Lack of promotion?
Coachee:	Well, that's only one aspect of this. I'm not saying that it's the one thing that has led to my dissatisfaction, but it certainly made me quite … well, angry, I guess. I have always given this organisation everything. From day one, I have been fully committed to this organisation. It's where I always wanted to work. I came here straight after college. My friends went on to more prestigious organisations, and they're really flying in their jobs. Every other day, one of them changes their LinkedIn status. Head of this, manager of that … And they're earning more now than I'd ever earn here. So, I guess I feel this organisation should reward me in the same way that they are being rewarded. But I do recognise that this organisation does not have as many opportunities for promotion. It's smaller …
Coach:	[Remains silent]
Coachee:	And because I was interested in being promoted, I have been investing extra time, even working on weekends. I finished a group project that I was leading by myself in order to meet a deadline. I mean, that's what is really frustrating. I put in all that effort! My manager does appreciate the work I do. And he did talk to me about the reasons that I was not successful in my application to be promoted. He is certainly right in some ways. There was only one position, and four of us had applied. Two of the group were rejected last year and have much more experience than I do. So, I can see … I can understand what happened, I guess.
Coach:	So what else is causing the frustration?
Coachee:	Well, I guess it is really all related to this. I was quite happy here until I got the rejection email. You know, the one that says, "It was a difficult decision", blah, blah. The frustrating thing is that my manager encouraged me to apply! I probably should have waited another year before applying. You know, every time I have a review meeting with my manager, it's all praise. But I'm not really sure now. Maybe he's just trying to keep me happy, you know? The other thing is that this is the only place I have ever worked. I don't know whether I'm just good in relation to this organisation,

	you know? Everyone here seemed to appreciate my work. And my colleagues are very supportive. They all think I should have been promoted. They don't understand it either.
Coach:	[remains silent]
Coachee:	But you know what? I think this rejection has really affected my perspective on this organisation. There are a few things that are annoying me, but, talking to you, I've realised that they are all related—in one way or another—to the rejection of my application for promotion. Apart from that, it's quite a good place to work. The chairman of the panel emailed me directly, offering feedback, but I haven't even replied to it. I probably should do that, and at least hear what he has to say. I am still angry, though. I do feel let down. And it's humiliating. My colleagues all know that I applied for a promotion. But there is actually one colleague of mine who also applied for it, who has been here five years longer than me. And he was rejected too.
Coach:	So, you're not the only one in this situation?
Coachee:	No. There's four of us in this situation. Having talked about it with you, I feel that I've probably over-reacted a bit. I don't want to make things worse. My relationship with my manager is more difficult now, but that's probably my fault because I'm blaming him for encouraging me to apply for this. And the chairman of the interview panel is the director of the company. Not responding to his email is probably not a good thing. I think I should probably talk to both of them before making any decisions. After all, this is the organisation that I'd always wanted to work for! And it still is, I guess. But I will explain how I'm feeling to my manager, and also listen to the director's feedback. Depending on that, I think I will decide my next steps. I want to keep my options open, though.

Valuing the coachee

Through the process of taking time to listen carefully, a coach can demonstrate that he or she values the coachee. In the increasing busyness of everyday life, it can seem that there are fewer opportunities for people to listen to one another. Having the full attention of the coach for between thirty minutes and two hours per session can feel like a real luxury. It is important, as mentioned above, that it is made clear that the coaching session is for the *coachee* to talk, think, and be listened to.

Try it out

People often appreciate someone taking time to listen. To see this in practice, why not try this out with someone you work with? The next time you see him or her, after an initial greeting, try asking, "So, how are things with you at the moment?" And then just listen without interrupting. Observe how people react to this.

Showing interest in the topic being discussed

There are many ways in which people can show interest in what others are saying. It is part of the coach's role to demonstrate that he or she is fully engaged in the conversation. This should be done in a genuine way. In other words, the coach should *be* interested in the topic, rather than *seem* interested. This is obviously quite a challenging idea. Many of us have probably developed ways to nod and look interested even when we are not very excited about the topic being discussed. In one-to-one conversations such as coaching, this will become obvious to the coachee very quickly, so it is important that we can demonstrate genuine interest in the topic.

For example

One of the authors was working with members of the senior management in a large organisation. One of the coachees brought a topic relating to data sharing within his institution and some of the challenges of sharing information between departments. The issue itself was very complicated and involved some very specific details and required significant legal knowledge to understand the difficulties that the institution was facing. In this situation, the topic itself was not of direct interest to the coach. Instead of directing interest towards the topic, the coach chose to show interest in the coachee and the ways in which he was trying to resolve the complex issue through structural changes and negotiation with colleagues.

Creating a "thinking space"

The quality of the listening by the coach contributes significantly to the creation of an environment that encourages new ideas and creative thinking (Kline, 1999). Through an alliance between an engaged coach and a committed coachee, it is possible to create a "thinking space" which will be fertile ground for insights and new ideas. When coachees feel genuinely listened to, and feel that their ideas are being appreciated by the coach in a non-judgmental way, it increases their own confidence in what they are saying and thinking. This positive perception of their own ability to come up with interesting ideas and insights will increase the chances of coachees finding their own solutions.

Building trust

Listening in a supportive and non-judgmental way is a key ingredient of an effective professional relationship or alliance. By listening intently and respectfully to their coachees, coaches are building the foundation of every successful coaching relationship: trust. Research into the effectiveness of one-to-one supportive conversations has identified that there is a correlation between the strength of a relationship and the likelihood of positive outcomes (de Haan, 2008; Grencavage & Norcross, 1990). Furthermore, it has been proposed that of all the variables within the control of the coach, it is the strength of the relationship that is the most significant. In other words, coaches should work hard to build trust with a coachee in order to strengthen the relationship, thereby increasing the likelihood of a positive outcome for the coachee.

Now that we have explored the purpose of listening when coaching, we will turn our attention to some of the practical skills required by coaches. As we have already mentioned, you will possess many of these skills already. It will simply be a case of sharpening these skills for use within coaching conversations.

The practical skills

At the very heart of listening in coaching is a genuine and respectful acceptance that the coaching conversation provides time and space for the *coachee* to think and speak. Having said this, there are a number of practical considerations that are helpful to review at this point.

1. Reduce the amount of time speaking

   For many people learning to become coaches, the most difficult first step is to simply reduce the amount of time they spend talking. Without realising it, many of us engage in daily conversations by listening briefly to the other person and then switching to preparing what we may say in response. Since it has been suggested that the coach should spend 80 to 90 per cent of his or her time listening, it becomes essential for the coach to be able to reduce the amount of time he or she spends speaking, thereby allowing more time for the coachee to express him- or herself.

In practice

It can be helpful to start by monitoring some of your everyday conversations. Make an estimate of how much time you spend speaking in comparison to listening. This may be different based on the person with whom you are having the conversation. With this skill, as with all of the others mentioned in this book, the first stage of development is raised self-awareness of your own strengths, tendencies, and preferences.

---

2. Remember the various purposes of listening

   In this chapter, we have proposed that there are different purposes for listening (in the context of coaching conversations):

   - Increasing the self-awareness of the coachee
   - Valuing the coachee
   - Showing interest in the topic
   - Creating "thinking spaces"
   - Building trust.

It is helpful to remember the various purposes. Coaches should be intentional about the use of the different coaching skills. For example, the coach should remember that the purpose of listening (in a coaching conversation) is not to find out about the coachee's situation or problem so that the coach can propose a solution. At the same time, coaches should remind themselves that the topic of the conversation should be driven by what is of interest to their coachees.

> ## In practice
>
> The next time you have a disagreement with someone, perhaps experiment with the notion of listening to the other's view or perspective fully before presenting your own thoughts. Often, high quality listening of this kind will demonstrate that you value the other person's opinion. It will also help to build trust between both parties, hopefully leading to a positive resolution.

3. Eye contact

   Although cultural variations must be taken into account, it is part of the coach's role to provide appropriate levels of eye contact. Being ready with eye contact is one of the best ways to demonstrate attentiveness. Coachees can make decisions about the extent to which they take advantage of the eye contact. Often coachees will look away as they are tackling challenging topics or formulating new ideas. However, when they look to the coach after their reflections, it is important that the coach is evidently still fully attentive.

> ## In practice
>
> Consider the appropriate use of eye contact within your society or culture. How can you use eye contact effectively in your coaching practice? Make some notes about how you will use eye contact in different coaching scenarios.

4. Body language

   Once again, cultural variations exist, so it is recommended that this is managed sensitively. The key point is that the coach should display open and welcoming body language, being aware of how he or she might be perceived by the coachee (see box below). It has been suggested that it is helpful, particularly in the early stages of a coaching conversation, to match your body language to that of the coachee. This helps to create rapport and can speed up the creation of a positive and trusting relationship.

> ## In practice
>
> The study of body language is not an exact science. However, awareness of body language and possible interpretations can support the coach in his or her role. Consider the table below that lists various types of body language and *possible* ways that we might interpret them. Remember that information that coaches gather from the body language of their coachees should only be used as *supplementary* information. For more information about body language, see *The Definitive Book of Body Language* (Pease & Pease, 2005).

Body language clues

Table 3.1. Body posture (adapted from van Nieuwerburgh, 2017).

Body posture	Possible interpretation
Coachee is leaning forward	Coachee may be looking forward to the discussion Coachee may be engaged in the topic of conversation Coachee may be impatient
Coachee is leaning backward	Coachee may feel comfortable within the relationship Coachee may be reluctant to discuss a particular topic
Coachee is sitting upright	Coachee may feel confident Coachee may not be relaxed

Table 3.2. Hands and fingers (adapted from van Nieuwerburgh, 2017).

Hands or fingers	Possible interpretation
Coachee's hand is clenched in a fist	Coachee may be nervous or afraid Coachee may be angry
Coachee is tapping his or her fingers	Coachee may be bored Coachee may be impatient
Coachee is biting his or her finger nails	Coachee may be anxious
Coachee's hand is on his or her chin	Coachee may be thinking Coachee may be evaluating the options
Coachee's hand or finger is covering his or her mouth	Coachee may not wish to share his or her thoughts Coachee may not believe what he or her is saying

(Continued)

Table 3.2. Continued.

Hands or fingers	Possible interpretation
Coachee's hand is on his or her forehead	Coachee may be embarrassed Coachee may be concerned or worried
Coachee is scratching his or her head	Coachee may be embarrassed Coachee may be thinking
Coachee touches his or her eyebrows	Coachee may be embarrassed Coachee may be trying to hide something
Coachee rubs his or her hands together	Coachee may be excited about the future Coachee may be anticipating a positive outcome

Table 3.3. Arms and legs (adapted from van Nieuwerburgh, 2017).

Arms and legs	Possible interpretation
Coachee's arms are crossed	Coachee may be feeling defensive Coachee may be uncomfortable discussing the topic
Coachee strokes his or her shoulder	Coachee may be comforting him- or herself Coachee may be lacking in confidence about the topic
Coachee's legs are crossed	Coachee may be feeling defensive Coachee may be uncomfortable discussing the topic
Coachee's legs are bouncing up and down	Coachee may be anxious Coachee may be feeling impatient

5. Energy levels

While it is important to be conscious of body language, it is also helpful to notice the energy levels of the coachee. Once again, matching energy levels can help to build rapport. For example, if the coachee is energetic and sitting forward, the coach could do the same, nodding and making encouraging noises and comments. However, if the coachee is fairly soft-spoken, and low in energy, the coach could sit back and listen quietly. This shows that the coach is sensitive to the coachee's emotions.

> ## In practice
>
> Think about your own energy levels throughout a typical day. Are there any consistent times when you have higher levels of energy than others? Or are there certain activities that you undertake which increase or decrease your level of energy? If you think of any patterns, make a note of these. In a coaching conversation, be aware of your own level of energy and the coachee's level of energy.

6. Allow for silences

   Conversations that include silences and quiet moments tend to encourage the creation of the "thinking spaces" we are exploring in this chapter. One very powerful way of demonstrating careful and respectful listening is to allow for some silences in the conversation. This means taking time before sharing your own thoughts after the coachee has stopped speaking. This shows that you are listening and thinking carefully about what the coachee has said.

> ## In practice
>
> How comfortable are you with silences? Think about whether you enjoy silences or quiet places. If you do, then you should use this in your coaching conversations. If you realise you prefer busy, noisy places and that you are uncomfortable with silences during conversations, you may wish to challenge yourself to appreciate quiet places. Take some time to go somewhere very quiet, and see if you can start to enjoy that kind of tranquility.

7. Do not judge

   In many situations in our lives, we may feel judged by others. Coaching should not be one of those situations. The most effective coaches do not judge their coachees. When coachees realise that their coach will not judge them, they are more likely to be honest about their thoughts and feelings. Maintaining a non-judgmental stance is another way of building a strong, trusting relationship between coach and coachee.

In practice

This may well be one of the most difficult things to do. As human beings we seem to be judging and making assumptions all the time. It is important for every coach to find a way of being able to set these judgments and assumptions to one side when working with coachees. Coaches should be alert to any beliefs that they hold about their coachees and ensure that these do not interfere in the ability to genuinely listen to the coachee and understand the coachee's view of the situation.

---

8. Withhold advice

   To ensure that you will be engaging in coaching rather than teaching or preaching, it is essential that you recognise that coaching is all about the coachee creating his or her own solutions, ideas, and future plans. If you accept this concept, then it becomes clear that there is no need for the coach to provide advice or suggestions. An effective coach should never provide answers. That is the job of the coachee.

In practice

This is often a very challenging concept, and many people who are interested in developing their coaching skills are driven by a desire to help others. That is why it can be so easy to get trapped into providing advice. As with some of the other skills, the first stage of developing this ability is to become aware of our tendency to give advice or provide solutions. Once we are aware of this, we can try to reduce the amount of advice we offer others. For example, a first step would be to respond to someone's request for advice by asking him or her what he or she thinks he or she should do.

---

9. Be comfortable with not knowing

   This is another challenging concept for many of us. Due to the way that we think and interact with others, it can be easy to assume that we "know" what someone will say. We can sometimes predict how a person may react in certain situations. In coaching, this is unhelpful.

This is because our expectation about what a person will say or how he or she might react might influence our understanding of the situation.

In practice

In coaching, it is essential that we try as much as possible to hear what the coachee is saying, rather than be distracted by our interpretation of the situation. To enhance this ability, simply be alert for your own tendency to believe that you know how others will react or what they will say. As a coach, it is important to try to adopt a curious stance rather than a knowing position.

---

10. Reduce distractions

    It is normal to be distracted when we are engaged in conversations. This is why it is highly recommended that coaching should be undertaken in places where there are relatively few distractions. This helps the coachee as much as the coach. It allows both parties to focus on what is important: the thinking process of the coachee.

In practice

This requires careful selection of meeting places for coaching. A small room without a telephone or other electronic devices would be ideal. It is also important that coach and coachee can discuss the topic without interruption from others. During the conversations, it is helpful if the coach does not sit facing a window, again reducing the risk of being distracted by what is taking place outside the room.

Concept of listening in the Noble Qur'an

Hearing includes three known degrees in physiology, which is mentioned in the Noble Qur'an. First, a person can have a sense of sound without understanding, like a newborn child who does not understand the meaning of words. The child can hear a sound but does not understand meaning. Another example of this is when a grazier calls animals to guide them. They do not understand what the grazier is saying, but simply hear a voice as is mentioned in the Noble Qur'an. God says: "The likeness of those who disbelieve is as the likeness of one who shouts to that which hears nothing, save a call and a cry; deaf, dumb, blind—they do not understand" (2:171).

وَمَثَلُ الَّذِينَ كَفَرُوا كَمَثَلِ الَّذِي يَنْعِقُ بِمَا لَا يَسْمَعُ إِلَّا دُعَاءً وَنِدَاءً ۚ صُمٌّ بُكْمٌ عُمْيٌ فَهُمْ لَا يَعْقِلُونَ - 2:171

Second, a person can have the sense of sound along with understanding. God says: "Are you then so eager that they should believe you, seeing there is a party of them that heard God's word, and then tampered with it, and that after they had comprehended it, wittingly?" (2:75).

وَقَدْ كَانَ فَرِيقٌ مِّنْهُمْ يَسْمَعُونَ كَلَامَ اللَّهِ ثُمَّ يُحَرِّفُونَهُ مِن بَعْدِ مَا عَقَلُوهُ وَهُمْ يَعْلَمُونَ - 2:75

Third, a person can have the sense of sound with understanding as well as conviction and faith. This is the highest degree of listening granted to the faithful. God says in the Noble Qur'an: "Answer only will those who hear; as for the dead, God will raise them up, then unto Him they will be returned" (6:36).

إِنَّمَا يَسْتَجِيبُ الَّذِينَ يَسْمَعُونَ ۚ - 6:36

These three meanings are compatible with what is known in the physiology of the sense of sound. The Noble Qur'an has differentiated between hearing, listening, and deep listening.

Hearing can be on purpose but may also happen inadvertently (without intention). God says in the Noble Qur'an: "When they hear idle talk, they turn away from it and say, 'We have our deeds, and you your deeds. Peace be upon [you]. We desire not the ignorant'" (28:55).

وَإِذَا سَمِعُوا اللَّغْوَ أَعْرَضُوا عَنْهُ - 28:55

In relation to listening with intent in order to benefit, God says: "And when We turned to thee a company of jinn giving ear to the Koran; and when they were in its presence they said, 'Be silent!' Then, when it was finished, they turned back to their people, warning" (46:29).

وَإِذْ صَرَفْنَا إِلَيْكَ نَفَرًا مِّنَ الْجِنِّ يَسْتَمِعُونَ الْقُرْآنَ - 46:29

The faithful are advised to use deep listening in relation to messages from the Noble Qur'an: "And when the Koran is recited, give you ear to it and be silent; haply so you will find mercy" (7:204).

وَإِذَا قُرِئَ الْقُرْآنُ فَاسْتَمِعُوا لَهُ وَأَنصِتُوا لَعَلَّكُمْ تُرْحَمُونَ - 7:204

Conclusion

In this chapter we have covered the importance of the skill of listening with purpose and related this to Islamic culture. It is a slightly more sophisticated way of listening, and it is the basis of strong and effective coaching relationships. When performed well, listening with purpose should make our coachees feel valued, appreciated, and more confident in their own abilities.

Try it out

One of the best ways of developing your coaching skills is to receive coaching for yourself. Why not find someone who would be willing to coach you? Experiencing first-hand what it is like to be listened to will make it easier for you to listen to others in the same way.

The importance of listening cannot be underestimated in Islam. Listening counts as the most important way of learning. According to the Noble Qur'an: "It is God who brought you forth from your mothers' wombs, and He appointed for you hearing, and sight, and hearts, that haply so you will be thankful" (16:78).

وَاللَّهُ أَخْرَجَكُم مِّن بُطُونِ أُمَّهَاتِكُمْ لَا تَعْلَمُونَ شَيْئًا وَجَعَلَ لَكُمُ السَّمْعَ وَالْأَبْصَارَ وَالْأَفْئِدَةَ لَعَلَّكُمْ تَشْكُرُونَ
16:78 -

CHAPTER FOUR

Asking powerful questions

Using questions in coaching

Similar to the skill of listening discussed in the previous chapter, the use of questions is also a commonly used conversational skill. Once again, coaching requires the intentional and skilful use of questioning in order to support positive outcomes for the coachee. This chapter will consider in detail the various purposes and applications of questioning within coaching conversations. We will start by considering a number of different types of questions, some of which are appropriate for coaching. Then we will focus on how coaches can use questions strategically and effectively with their coachees. Finally, we will propose how questions can drive the conversational process.

Types of question

In coaching-related training, it is often suggested that there are four types of questions worth learning (open questions, closed questions, leading questions, and multiple questions) (adapted from van Nieuwerburgh, 2017).

Open questions

Open questions refer to those that cannot be answered with a simple "yes" or "no" response. In other words, they are "open" because they allow for a very broad range of answers. This is important for coaching because the intention is to create a space for the coachee to explore his or her thinking. Open questions encourage this. Furthermore, by their very nature, they invite the coachee to provide a full response, rather than a brief, one-word answer. If we recall that we are aiming for conversations where the coachee is doing 80–90 per cent of the talking, it becomes clear that open questions are essential.

In practice

It is useful for coaches to practise using open questions in everyday conversations. The best open questions can start with the words "How" or "What".

For example, here are four alternative questions:

Do you think it will be useful for you to practise this in everyday conversations?

Or

How do you think it would be helpful for you to practise this in everyday conversations?

Or

What would be the benefits of practising this in everyday conversations?

Or

Will you be able to practise this in everyday conversations?

Although the following sentence is not a question, it can be used as an alternative to an open question.

"Tell me more about ..."

For example, "Tell me more about the idea of practising the use of open questions."

Although "Why" could also be the start of an open question, it is advisable to be cautious when using the word in coaching conversations.

Questions starting with "why" can be experienced as judgmental or critical. For example, if a coachee were asked, "Why have you not been able to achieve your goal?", it might be interpreted as criticism. However, the same question could be asked in the following way, reducing the chance of misinterpretation: "What has stopped you from achieving your goal?" Furthermore, "why" questions can elicit defensiveness. Imagine that you were asked, "Why are you reading this book while seated?" Such a question almost demands a defence or an explanation.

So, the use of appropriate open questions is necessary for effective coaching conversations. We are not suggesting that coaches must only ask open questions. Rather, we are suggesting that the coach should be able to differentiate between different types of questions. As we will discuss below, open questions are more helpful in certain situations.

Closed questions

To put it simply, closed questions are those that can be answered with one word, usually "Yes" or "No", but also a number. Although this type of question can have distinct disadvantages when it comes to encouraging the coachee to do most of the talking, there are situations when such questions are helpful. This will be explored further in this chapter.

In practice

Closed questions start with the following words

- Do
- Did
- When
- Where
- Is
- Are
- Have.

For example:
"Do you think you will be able to overcome this challenge?"
"Did you know that you would be asked to take on this project?"
"When will you receive your certificate?"

"Where will the interview take place?"

"Is it realistic to expect that you will complete this task within two weeks?"

"Are there any opportunities for training offered by your organisation?"

"Have you ever been involved in a similar situation?"

It would be a good exercise to make a mental note of how many closed questions and open questions you ask during a typical conversation. An awareness of your personal style will definitely support you to develop your own coaching practice.

As we will see later in this chapter, closed questions are also helpful during coaching conversations. Ideally, coaches will be able to use both closed and open questions tactically to have effective and purposeful conversations with their coachees.

Leading questions

While both closed and open questions are welcome in coaching conversations, leading questions are to be avoided at all costs. A leading question is one that implies a "preferred" response. This means that the phrasing of the question encourages the coachee to answer in a particular way. For example, "Have you thought about finding another job?" may seem to be an innocent closed question. However, this is a suggestion pretending to be a question. It contains a suggestion ("Think about finding another job") within it.

Newly trained coaches often find themselves drawn to leading questions because they are trying to remember not to give advice or provide solutions. So, while they have managed not to say, for example, "I think you should talk to your manager about this" (advice), they end up asking, "What do you think about talking to your manager about this situation?" (leading question).

Leading questions are to be avoided because they can be considered manipulative. They tend to put thoughts into our coachees' minds. A clear piece of advice would be preferable to a suggestion hidden within a seemingly open or closed question.

> ## In practice
>
> With leading questions, we often do not realise that we are asking them. So, it is helpful to record yourself having a conversation with someone, listening to the audio, and seeing if you are asking leading questions. As always, the first step is to raise your own awareness. If you do find that you are asking leading questions, the next step would be to try to reduce the number of such questions. Ultimately, you will want to ensure that you do not ask any leading questions when coaching.

Multiple questions

The phrase "multiple questions" refers to the situations in which a person asks a number of questions consecutively without allowing the other person to respond in between. This is unhelpful in coaching conversations as multiple questions can overload the coachee and lead to some important questions remaining unanswered.

> ## In practice
>
> Here is a sample conversation to elucidate the reason that multiple questions should be avoided.
>
> Coachee: I'm not sure whether I should apply for the new job.
> Coach: What is making you uncertain about this? Do you think that the job will be too challenging? ... Or is it more a case of worrying about what your colleagues think? Are you being influenced by them?
> Coachee: No, I don't think so. My colleagues are very supportive. So, it's not about being influenced by them. No.
>
> In the excerpt above, the coach asked a number of questions that overwhelmed the coachee. As is often the case in these situations, the coachee will pick one question to answer. The real reasons for the uncertainty are left unexplored.
>
> Multiple questions should also be avoided because they detract from the impression that the coach is asking thoughtful and purposeful questions.

It is recommended that coaches develop the skill of asking single questions, pausing at the end of each to allow the coachee to respond. If the coach has asked a question that is too difficult to answer, or the coachee does not fully understand the query, the coachee will ask the coach to reframe the question. This means that there is no need for the coach to follow up with a "better question", even if this pops into the coach's head while asking the first question. Best practice would suggest that the coach should simply ask the initial question and allow the coachee to answer it.

Now that we have examined the various *types* of questions, we will turn our attention to the purposeful use of questions within coaching conversations. While it is important for a coach's questions to follow on from the coachee's contributions, the coach should also be aware of the *purpose* of asking certain questions.

The purpose of questions

First, questions can be used to clarify. Clarification questions are usually closed questions that give the coach an opportunity to check his or her own understanding of what has been shared. This use of questioning can improve a coach's understanding of the coachee's situation. At the same time, it will also demonstrate to the coachee that the coach is trying hard to understand.

For example

Coachee: So, I always inform my managers as well as my colleagues in the central office. And when they have any comments, I usually take the time to consider them. In this situation, I think that they may have not realised that I had already added these thoughts to the new proposal.

Coach: OK. Are you referring to your managers or your colleagues?

Coachee: It's my colleagues. My managers know that I have updated the proposal. Now that I think about it, my colleagues gave me feedback, but they don't know that I've taken their ideas into account.

Second, it is sometimes helpful to support coachees to clarify their own thinking. This is particularly the case when they seem to be uncertain about their own interpretation of a certain situation. Again, this is likely to be a closed question and should be asked when the coach feels that the coachee would benefit from exploring the issue further.

For example

Coachee: I'm not sure about this. I think that we should probably move forward on this project even though it's probably not the best solution. The staff are not convinced, but the project manager is very competent. And I think he will be able to complete the project ...

Coach: So, is this project worth pursuing despite the challenges?

There will also be moments in the conversation when it will be helpful for the coachee to explore the situation further. This kind of exploration can often help the coachee to see the current situation from a different perspective. One of the aims of coaching is to support coachees to be able to see things differently or think in a new way.

Using open questions is the best way of helping the coachee to explore the topic more deeply. It is important that the coach is not leading the coachee towards a particular line of thinking. The open questions should emerge from the coach's curiosity.

For example

Coachee: Ever since he has become my manager, our relationship at work has changed ...

Coach: How has it changed?

Coachee: Well ... I don't know exactly. It just feels different.

Coach: What's different?

Coachee: I guess it's just that we don't talk as much as before.

Coach: How come?

Coachee: For a start, he's moved to another office. And he doesn't seem to have much time for me. But, to be fair, he does now manage the whole team.

Coach: And how does that change things, do you think?

Coachee: I guess he now has more people that he needs to talk to regularly. It could be that he doesn't want people to think that he's treating me differently ...

Finally, questions can be used to challenge coachees. As coaches, one of our roles is to support coachees to achieve more than they are currently achieving. This will sometimes involve pushing coachees out of their comfort zone. This can be done through the purposeful use of questions. By drawing attention to certain patterns or beliefs, a coach can help coachees to focus on what is going to make a real difference.

For example

Coachee: I know that I want to get promoted, but I never seem to have the courage to mention this to my manager. Some of my friends are completing IT courses, because this is essential for our promotion. But they take so much time, and I really don't want to spend all my time working or studying. I've been doing the same job for five years now. I think it's time for something to change.

Coach: You have said that you won't mention it to your manager, and you're not prepared to take an IT course. So what has to change for you to get a promotion?

The status of questions in the Noble Qur'an

The Noble Qu'ran gives great attention to questions. They are considered to be one of the most important means of learning. Moreover, they are tools for accessing the knowledge and facts that learners desire to know. First, let us note that God says: "And We sent none before thee, but men to whom We made revelation—question the People of the Remembrance, if you do not know—" (21:7).

وَمَا أَرْسَلْنَا قَبْلَكَ إِلَّا رِجَالًا نُوحِي إِلَيْهِمْ ۚ فَاسْأَلُوا أَهْلَ الذِّكْرِ إِن كُنتُمْ لَا تَعْلَمُونَ - 21:7

Asking questions of scholars and experts was a method used in the Noble Qur'an to prove the truth of faith.

In another passage God says: "So, if thou art in doubt regarding what We have sent down to thee, ask those who recite the Book before thee. The truth has come to thee from thy Lord; so be not of the doubters" (10:94).

فَإِن كُنتَ فِي شَكٍّ مِّمَّا أَنزَلْنَا إِلَيْكَ فَاسْأَلِ الَّذِينَ يَقْرَءُونَ الْكِتَابَ مِن قَبْلِكَ ۚ لَقَدْ جَاءَكَ الْحَقُّ مِن رَّبِّكَ فَلَا تَكُونَنَّ مِنَ الْمُمْتَرِينَ - 10:94

The importance of questions in the Sunnah

The Sunnah gave great emphasis to the importance of questions. This can be noted in the Prophet Muhammad's (peace be upon him) use of questions. He used a particular style of conversation as a way of educating his companions. For example, the Prophet (peace be upon him) encourages his companions to ask questions: Abu Huraira (may God be pleased with him), recounts that: "The Messenger of God, peace be upon him, said 'Ask me' and then came a man who sat down at his knees. This man said: 'Messenger of God, what is Islam?' The Prophet (peace be upon him) replied: 'There is no true deity but God, performing prayers, supporting the needy, fasting during the Month of Ramadan …'" (Sahih Muslim 10—Book 1, Hadith 7).

This Hadith highlights the ideas of encouraging people to ask questions based on their desire to learn and the use of dialogue for people to learn more about their religion. In one case, the Prophet Muhammad (peace be upon him) uses a question to engage his listeners: "Amongst the trees, there is a tree, the leaves of which do not fall and is like a Muslim. Tell me the name of that tree" (Sahih al-Bukhari 61—Book 3, Hadith 3).

*   *   *

Ultimately, the two skills we have considered so far (listening with purpose and asking powerful questions) lie at the heart of effective coaching practice. In both cases, the intention is to create the context in which the coachee will feel valued and the conditions that will encourage the coachee to develop his or her own strategies and solutions. At first glance, it may seem that asking questions is the more "active" of the skills. However, the effective coach should consider both listening and asking questions as "active" interventions.

CHAPTER FIVE

Summarising and paraphrasing

A s we have discussed from the outset, coaching is about providing a respectful and thoughtful space for people to reflect openly and come to their own, well-considered conclusions. The quality of the coaching relationship is the most important factor in creating this type of environment.

We have already discussed some of the key skills needed by the coach. First, the ability to listen actively, being an "interested listener" as we have mentioned earlier in this book (Chapter Three). We have also argued that the quality of listening provided by the coach can have a direct impact on the quality of thinking in the coachee. Second, the key intervention of the coach is the use of thought-provoking questions. We have already suggested that coaches need to be able to ask questions to support the coachee's exploration of the topic (Chapter Four). We now turn our attention to two related skills: summarising and paraphrasing. As we have seen, it is essential that the coach *demonstrates* that he or she is listening to the coachee. In addition to active listening, these two skills can provide evidence to the coachee that he or she is being listened to.

Defining the terms

In English, the terms "summarising" and "paraphrasing" are similar and sometimes used interchangeably to suggest forms of capturing information and reflecting it back to someone. However, in coaching, the two related skills serve different purposes and should be studied separately.

In coaching, the term "summarise" has the following key features:

1. To summarise is to present back to the coachee what he or she has said in a condensed or shortened form.
2. A summary is an abridged review of what the coachee has said.
3. In summarising, the coach will necessarily be editing out some of the information that has been shared.

In contrast, paraphrasing involves:

1. Rewording and presenting back what the coachee has said, but not in abbreviated form.
2. Restating the coachee's point using similar words or phrases.
3. Expressing the same meaning as the coachee using the same or slightly different words.

We can see that the only key similarity relates to the "presenting back" of data to the coachee. So, in that sense, summarising and paraphrasing fulfil a similar function and can both *demonstrate* to the coachee that the coach has been listening intently to him or her. However, each has a different function. These functions will be explored below.

Paraphrasing when coaching

During coaching conversations, the coach can paraphrase in order to demonstrate that he or she has been listening. One way of using paraphrasing in coaching is to play back what the coachee has just said, using a mixture of similar or identical words.

> ## For example
>
> Coachee: I am often in situations in which I think I *should* say something about my colleague's behaviour—but something prevents me from doing so.
>
> Coach: So, you find yourself in situations when you think you *should* say something about what your colleague does, but something prevents you.

When paraphrasing, we are not shortening or abbreviating anything, so it should be about the same length as the coachee's statement. When coachees hear back the words that they have just used, this provides them with evidence that the coach has been listening to them. It may be surprising, but coachees often behave as if they have heard what is being said for the first time. It seems that hearing someone else saying what they have just said gives it a different flavour. Sometimes, coachees say things such as, "Yes, that's exactly right. That's what is interesting."

In some cases, coaches may even want to simply "mirror" what a coachee says. In this case, coaches repeat, word for word, what a coachee has said. This can be used to allow the coachee to "hear" what he or she has just said, or to emphasise a certain point that is worth reflecting on.

> ## For example
>
> Coachee: I know that there will be pressure for me to apply for the role of regional manager when it becomes available. I guess my colleagues will expect me to go for it. And I think that I might be able to get the job. In some ways, this is the job that I always wanted ...
>
> Coach: So, in some ways, this is the job you have always wanted?
>
> Coachee: Yes. It's true. Only in *some* ways, though. And this was what I might have wanted for myself when I started in this company. But now, things are a bit different. I have a family, and I already feel that I spend too much time at work. This job will require much more effort—and certainly more travel ...

Of course, being able to reflect back almost exactly what the coachee has said provides clear and unambiguous evidence of careful listening. So, paraphrasing and mirroring are important skills for a coach to have and to use during coaching conversations. They can be used to build rapport, as coachees are more likely to feel an affinity to people who "speak their language".

So, paraphrasing or mirroring should be used to provide evidence of accurate listening and also when it may be important to highlight a particular point. At times, the coach may think that it could be helpful for the coachee to "hear" what he or she has just said, but from the coach. The intentional use of paraphrasing can impact positively on the coaching conversation and on the relationship between the coach and the coachee.

Summarising when coaching

In addition to paraphrasing, summarising is an essential skill for coaches. It serves a number of functions over and above providing evidence to a coachee that he or she is being accurately and actively listened to. Summarising can achieve the following outcomes:

1. Provides evidence that the coach is interested and trying to understand.
2. Allows the coachee to correct misunderstandings or misinterpretation.
3. Allows the coachee to get a perception of how his or her thoughts might be understood by others.
4. Focuses attention on a particular aspect and creates opportunities for the coach to move the conversation forward.

Like paraphrasing, summarising demonstrates that the coach is attentive and has been listening carefully, especially when the coach's summary aligns with the coachee's own understanding of the situation.

Coachee: I am at an important point in my career. I think I have to make a decision soon. I have been contacted by a couple of other banks who will be opening branches in this city. I think that I can easily get a job as branch manager with at least two other banks. I know a few people there, and they've told me that I'd be exactly the kind of candidate that they would be looking for. And I think the pay will be better. At the same time, my own organisation is growing. It's a well-established bank, and its head office for the region is based here. And people know me here. I have built up an excellent reputation and it would be a shame to start again, if you know what I mean. My managers know me—and I have a great team of people around me. There is a good possibility that I will be promoted internally—but I won't know about this until September, when I will have missed my chance to apply for the branch manager jobs at the other banks. That's the real challenge, you see.

Coach: So it sounds like you're feeling that you need to make a decision. On the one hand, there may be an opportunity for you to become a branch manager for one or two new banks opening in the city. On the other, you think that it might make more sense for you to see if you will be promoted internally, based on your reputation within your current organisation. But if you wait for the chance of an internal promotion, you may have missed your chance to apply for the branch manager roles. Is that about right?

Coachee: Yes, exactly. This is the situation—and now is the time to make a decision and stick with it.

Summarising is also a great way of checking that both the coach and the coachee are communicating effectively. Because summarising requires some interpretation in order to condense the subject matter, it can highlight differences in understanding. That is why it is very important for the coach to be tentative when providing a summary. Phrases such as "Let me see if I have understood you correctly" or "Can I just check that I have got this right?" can be helpful before providing the summary. It is also good practice to finish the summary by inviting the coachee to comment: "Is that about right?" or "Am I on the right track?" or "Have I presented this fairly?" If the coachee agrees with the summary, this gives both parties the reassurance that they are talking about the same thing. If the coachee disagrees, then it has been a useful opportunity to correct any misunderstanding.

> **Coachee:** I am at an important point in my career. I think I have to make a decision soon. I have been contacted by a couple of other banks who will be opening branches in this city. I think that I can easily get a job as branch manager with at least two other banks. I know a few people there, and they've told me that I'd be exactly the kind of candidate that they would be looking for. And I think the pay will be better. At the same time, my own organisation is growing. It's a well-established bank, and its head office for the region is based here. And people know me here. I have built up an excellent reputation and it would be a shame to start again, if you know what I mean. My managers know me—and I have a great team of people around me. There is a good possibility that I will be promoted internally—but I won't know about this until September, when I will have missed my chance to apply for the branch manager jobs at the other banks. That's the real challenge, you see.
>
> **Coach:** So it sounds like you are aware that you would be successful in getting a branch manager role in one of the new banks opening in the city. But you're not prepared to leave your own organisation at the moment. Is that about right?
>
> **Coachee:** Well, not exactly. It's not guaranteed to get the branch manager role—and I'm a bit unsure about whether to stay in my current organisation or take a new opportunity now.
>
> **Coach:** Oh, I see. So the real question is about timing?
>
> **Coachee:** Yes. If there were some way to know my chances of promotion in September, that would really help me to make a decision.

In this case, the summarising demonstrates that the coach is trying hard to understand, and it also allows the coach to align his or her understanding to that of the coachee.

Alternatively, summarising can sometimes provide the coachee with a glimpse of how his or her thinking might be understood by others, giving him or her a helpful insight into the impact it may have on colleagues, family, or friends.

Coachee:	I don't really like to socialise at work and some people have started to comment about that. They joke about it, but I think that there is more to it than that. They say, "You are too important to have time for us," or "You should book an appointment one year in advance to see him for a coffee." But the truth is, I like to keep my business life and my personal life quite separate. I really like working, and my colleagues are great. We have a good time at work—but I don't really consider them to be friends. I have many friends already, and they are all really close friends— we've been friends from childhood. I also have a very big and caring family. We spend a lot of time together. For example, my sister is always coming round in the evening with her children. And all of the children, cousins, nieces, like to spend time together with us on the weekends. So between my friends and family, most of my free time is taken. I do have time for my colleagues, but only during working hours. That's why I don't ever go for a coffee or lunch with work colleagues—and I certainly don't have time for weddings and social events that take even longer! My time is precious and I have to use it carefully—and of course I am going to dedicate the free time that I have to the people who are most valuable to me—my family and my childhood friends.
Coach:	So it seems to me that there is a conflict between what your colleagues expect from you and how you like to manage the relationship between your work life and your personal life. Your colleagues think that you're too busy to see them outside work—and in some ways you are. If you have free time, you don't want to spend it with work colleagues—you prefer to focus on your friends and family. Have I got that right?
Coachee:	Yes—but when you say it like that, it makes me sound a bit unfriendly … I don't mean to make my colleagues feel that they are not important to me.

In this case, hearing back a summary has raised awareness about how the coachee *might* be perceived by others. There are times when this could be helpful and provide some useful insights about the perceptions of others. It is therefore important that coaches try to remain as objective as possible when summarising. They should not *try* to present information in a way that influences the coachee to respond in one way or another. The coach should simply play back and condense the information so that the coachee can hear (in a different voice) an independent interpretation of what has just been discussed.

Finally, summarising can also be used to manage the process of the coaching conversation. Skilful use of summaries can help to make the coaching conversation move forward in a timely and focused way. When a coach uses summarising in this way, he or she can turn attention to a particular aspect of what the coachee has said in order to highlight some positive aspects, identify a topic that may need further exploration, or move the conversation towards the next stage of the coaching process (that will be discussed in Chapter Seven).

There will be times in coaching conversations when the coach may think that the coachee might want to explore a certain belief or perception more deeply. In these situations, the coach can summarise in such a way that highlights the importance of that belief or perception.

Coachee:	I have been working in this organisation for ten years, and I have only been promoted once. And that was eight years ago! I don't really understand why. I've never liked my manager, and I think he doesn't know how hard I work. I don't think he even cares whether I work hard or not. In his mind, as long as I do my work and I don't complain, that's all that matters. Every time we have a performance review meeting, I raise the issue of promotion—and it's obvious he doesn't want to talk about it. He's always talking about my "objectives" and "key performance indicators". I don't want to talk about that. It's so frustrating, and he is the one who has to agree my promotion. I don't think he'll ever do that—so I don't know what to do. I cannot work harder, and anyway, I am not motivated the way I used to be.
Coach:	Let me see if I have understood you correctly. Even though you work hard, you don't think that this is recognised by your manager. You've raised the issue of promotion, but he seems more interested in talking about practical, everyday objectives rather than your long-term career. It seems like the relationship with your manager is not working, and this is affecting your motivation and chances of promotion. Does that sum it up?
Coachee:	Yes, I think so. The relationship is just not working. Something has to change, otherwise I am starting to lose my motivation, and that is sure to affect my work.

At other times, if the coachee seems to be focusing only on the negatives, it can be helpful to balance out the positives and the negatives when summarising.

Coachee:	I don't think I have what it takes to be a leader. I think I'm too honest at times. And I hate conflict, so I am always trying to keep people happy. This can be counterproductive, and I think some of my team take advantage of this. We have recently launched a new project, but people aren't very committed and I am not sure if we will be able to deliver it. If we don't, our vice president will start to ask questions.
Coach:	It sounds like it has been a tough time for you recently. You're trying to be honest and you are interested in keeping your people happy. Not everyone appreciates this, and you are worried that you might need to change your personal style if you are to deliver the new project. Is that about right?
Coachee:	Yes. I don't want to change who I am completely, but my leadership style has to be adapted if we are going to deliver this project successfully.

Finally, we must remember that one of the coach's responsibilities is to manage the conversation. There will certainly be occasions when the coach will need to move the coachee onto a different phase of the conversation.

Coachee:	There are just too many variables, and I'm really not sure what to do next. I'm not sure whether I will still be living here; I am not sure whether I will have successfully passed my project management course; and I don't know how my family would feel about me living in Dubai. This is the confusing thing for me. I feel that I'm trying to make a decision without any of the information I need. It may just be best to wait …
Coach:	So, you still have a number of variables you should consider. You don't have enough information to make a final decision. What do you think you can do in the meantime?

In the above example, the coach has minimised the complexity of the situation by focusing attention on the fact that the coachee may not have the information he or she needs in order to make a final decision. This moves the conversation to a discussion about what the coachee *can* do until further information becomes available.

Using paraphrasing and summarising when coaching

In this chapter we have considered the use of two related skills when coaching. Both can be used effectively to demonstrate to coachees that they are being listened to. Paraphrasing does this by reflecting back to coachees what they have said through similar words and ideas that convey the same meaning. This can also be done by summarising the key points of what the coachee has said. In addition to this, summarising has other uses too. Summarising is a good way for the coach to check his or her understanding of what has been said. Effective summarising can highlight particular aspects of what the coachee has said. This can be used to focus more intentionally on positives.

We will now turn our attention to another set of coaching-related skills: giving and receiving feedback.

CHAPTER SIX

Giving and receiving feedback

Although some people would argue that giving feedback is not the primary role of a coach, it is often helpful if the coach does provide feedback to the coachee. Feedback can be especially useful if a lack of information is getting in the way of the coachee's success (van Nieuwerburgh, 2017). In this book, we propose that it is important for coaches to be able to give feedback as well as receive feedback.

Feedback can be provided in a number of ways, as we will see below. However, the conditions in which feedback is given plays an important role in ensuring that the information is accepted and taken on board.

Why is it difficult to give and receive feedback?

Time for personal reflection

Would you prefer to give negative feedback to someone or to receive negative feedback from someone? Please think carefully about this. Can you think of examples when you had to give negative feedback? How did that compare to when you received negative feedback from someone else?

Some people would rather receive negative feedback than give negative feedback to others. Either way, this suggests that there are some complexities surrounding the giving and receiving of feedback in our societies. So what makes it difficult? It may be helpful to think of "feedback" as information. At its most simple, feedback is "information"—and giving feedback involves one person (feedback provider) offering information to another person (feedback recipient).

So far, there are no difficulties. Human beings are competent at transmitting information in this way. However, the complexity emerges from the dynamics of the relationship. When one person sits in judgment over another, a power imbalance becomes apparent. If care is not taken, the feedback provider can seem to be criticising the feedback recipient. This means that when giving negative feedback to another person, this should be taken into account. The feedback provider should do whatever is possible to ensure that the relationship does not feel too imbalanced by the feedback recipient. This can be done by:

- Finding out what type of feedback the feedback recipient would like to receive
- Asking the feedback recipient's permission to provide feedback
- Maintaining a position of humility throughout the conversation.

The second complexity comes from the "information" itself. If the information seems to be biased, inaccurate, or based on opinion, it is possible for the feedback recipient to reject the information. It is the responsibility of the feedback provider to deliver accurate and helpful information. The chances of this can be increased by:

- Ensuring that the feedback is based on facts
- Avoiding generalisations or opinions
- Not using emotional language or exaggeration.

The final and most complex of the challenges comes from our natural defensiveness as human beings. We tend to want to protect ourselves from "attack", so it is natural that we put up some defences when we think that we may be criticised. Often, people are advised not to take feedback "personally"—but this is unreasonably difficult. If someone gives us feedback about the way we do something or the way we are, it *is* personal! So, even if the power balance is managed effectively and the information is delivered in an accurate and helpful way, the feedback recipient is still likely to become defensive. This means that although the information may be "sent" accurately and clearly by a feedback provider, it may not be received by the feedback recipient in that way. For the information to be received and acted upon, it is essential that the feedback recipient is open to the information. The best way of increasing the chances of this are:

- Creating a safe and encouraging climate
- Ensuring that the coachee feels respected
- Demonstrating that *you* are open to feedback.

Of course, the "safe and encouraging climate" where the "coachee feels respected" is the coaching conversation. Good coaching conversations underpinned by an effective professional relationship between a coach and a coachee should be such an environment. That is why coaching is an ideal opportunity for providing feedback to the coachee.

Time for personal reflection

Can you think of a time that you received feedback that was very difficult to accept at first—but later you were grateful for having had the honest feedback?

As mentioned above, it will be important for the coach to demonstrate an openness to feedback. In order to do this, the coach should request feedback about his or her effectiveness as a coach. It is good practice to ask for feedback at the end of every coaching conversation. And, of course, the coach will need to remember the complexities related to feedback and manage any defensiveness that he or she may feel. This means accepting both positive and negative feedback with openness and gratitude. It would not be appropriate, especially in these circumstances, to try to argue with the coachee about his or her feedback!

What type of feedback can a coach provide?

There are three main types of feedback that a coach can provide to a coachee. First, the coach can provide feedback about what happens during a coaching conversation. This is the most common source of feedback in most types of coaching. Second, the coach can provide the coachee with feedback based on data that has already been collected, such as reports from psychometric tests or 360 degree appraisals. Third, the coach can actually observe the coachee in his or her workplace and provide feedback about what he or she noticed.

1. Feedback about what happens during a coaching conversation
   The coach is ideally placed to provide the coachee with "real time" feedback about what happens within the coaching conversation. As the coach will be attentive and observant during the coaching conversation, he or she will be able to notice details about how the coachee reacts to certain topics. The coach may also be able to ascertain how the coachee prefers to manage situations or deal with certain types of challenges. There are also times when it may be helpful for the coach to reflect back the facial expressions or body language of the coachee.

Coachee: I don't know, but I quite like the idea of organising such a large event. I think I'd like the complex planning process—and the thought of producing something on that scale ...

Coach: I noticed that you sat up straight and were more energised when you were talking about this event.

Coachee: Really? I guess I am quite excited about the idea. I think it would make me proud to do something like this. And it would be a new challenge for me!

---

2. Feedback based on questionnaires or evaluations
   The use of psychometric or personality questionnaires is quite common in coaching (Passmore, 2008). There is a good connection between coaching and such questionnaires because both are interested in raising self-awareness. Most of these questionnaires are now completed online. Some focus on leadership abilities, others on personality types, resilience, mental toughness, character strengths, etc. Almost all these questionnaires result in detailed reports about the individual.
   360 degree questionnaires are also commonly used in organisations, especially when focusing on the development of managers or leaders. Questionnaires are sent out to a range of people who should represent the entire breadth of colleagues of a manager or leader

(that is why it is called a 360 degree survey—it includes respondents from the full circle of people around a manager or leader). This tool provides an anonymised report that collates the answers of all the respondents. It is hoped that this information about how a manager is perceived by others can be useful for the development and career planning of the manager.

The reports from any of the questionnaires mentioned above can form the basis of a good coaching conversation. When using such reports, it is usually helpful if the coachee has carefully considered the report before coming to the coaching session. It is recommended that the coachee sends the report to the coach beforehand, so that the coach will be familiar with the report prior to the coaching conversation.

Although the conversation should be led by the coachee as in any other type of coaching, it is possible in these situations for the coach to also provide evidence-based feedback from the report or highlight particular aspects for discussion.

For example (360 degree questionnaire)

Coachee: I'm not really sure why people have commented on my "kindness" as a leader. It's not something that I demonstrate at work, although I am very kind to my family.

Coach: Well, I notice that one of the written comments mentions that you give people time off for special family occasions, even if they don't request it.

Coachee: That's true. I don't see it as kindness, but you're right. That might explain it. I do it to keep the team motivated, but also because I think that having a good family life is important for everyone.

Giving feedback following observation

Less common is the idea of inviting the coach to observe the coachee in the workplace. However, this can be a very powerful way of becoming aware of how a manager or leader is perceived at work, and can provide valuable insights. In this case, the coach could be invited to the coachee's workplace to follow him or her through a typical working day. For example, the coach could attend a team meeting facilitated by the coachee or a presentation delivered by the coachee. The coach would take a discreet position during these events and then meet with the coachee afterwards to discuss improvements or observations.

Once again, it is important to remember two things. First, the coachee should lead the conversation and this should not turn into a performance review meeting. Second, the complexities of giving and receiving feedback should be remembered. The coachee may feel vulnerable having been "observed" by someone who was taking notes. So, the coach might start by asking the coachee about his or her performance during the observation. This can be followed up by asking the coachee which aspects of his or her behaviour or performance he or she would like to receive feedback about. As usual, the coach's primary role is to support the thinking of the coachee, so the conversation should be characterised by many questions and active listening from the coach, with the coachee doing most of the reflection and analysis about the implications of any feedback provided. As stated above, all feedback should be based on facts and observation, rather than opinion and generalisation.

An alternative, more cost-effective approach to this is through the use of video recording. According to a leading expert in the field of coaching, the use of video can have a significant impact on professional development (Knight, 2014). In this scenario, the coachee would be videotaped when undertaking certain professional roles (managing a project, leading a team meeting, giving a presentation, advising a colleague). The coachee would then have time to study the video recordings by him- or herself, and perhaps take some notes about what he or she notices. When the coachee is ready to discuss what has been observed, a meeting with the coach is scheduled. Both parties then watch the video together, discussing any issues or questions that arise. Again, the coachee should take the lead in the conversation, with the coach asking questions and providing his or her own comments about what he or she has observed by watching the video.

By organising it in this way, the coachee has time to reflect on his or her behaviours and may be less self-conscious when watching the video with the coach. The coach, who will be seeing the video for the first time, will bring a fresh, impartial perspective. The strength of this approach is that the "evidence" is there in front of both the coach and the coachee, whereas when the coachee is observed by the coach, there is a possibility of disagreement about what actually occurred.

Some tips about giving feedback

There are a number of tips to keep in mind when giving feedback during coaching conversations (van Nieuwerburgh, 2017).

1. Avoid watering down feedback
   - When giving someone feedback about improvements, it is unhelpful to water it down to make it acceptable to the recipient. Attempts to make feedback acceptable can confuse the recipient. It is better in these situations to give the feedback clearly and accurately.
   - Example of watered-down feedback: "You can sometimes come across as, you know, a little bit … well you're not as friendly to others as you are to your university friends. So, you're friendly to a certain extent—and that's probably enough for most people. But maybe not everyone?"
2. Avoid "sugarcoating" negative feedback
   - Sugarcoating refers to the practice of making feedback acceptable to a recipient by surrounding the feedback with positive information— the way that some medicines are coated with a sweet exterior to make the medicine nicer to swallow. As with watering down feedback, sugarcoating can lead to confusion and mixed messages. Usually, this type of sugarcoating means that the feedback provider says something positive at the outset, then gives the "real" feedback (or medicine) and then says something positive to finish with. That way, the feedback recipient will have had a positive start and a positive end to the interaction.
   - Example of sugarcoating: "I really think you are such an important member of our sales team—probably one of the best salespeople we've had here. We do sometimes hear, though, that one or two customers complain about what they consider to be 'aggressive' tactics and rudeness. But that's only a small minority of our customers. For the most part, you seem to be very enthusiastic and ambitious. I am sure that you will be the top salesperson again this year!"
3. Provide clear and specific feedback
   - When giving feedback, remember that we are trying to present information to the recipient that will help him or her to improve. Therefore, it is helpful to be quite clear and specific about the feedback that you are giving.

- For example: "I noticed that you stopped paying attention to the customer when she said that she was 'only looking'. You even walked away from her to talk to another customer before the conversation was finished. That kind of behaviour often leads to customer complaints."

4. Consider the ratio of positive to negative feedback you give to others
   - According to some research (Fredrickson & Losada, 2005), people perform better when they are given more positive feedback than negative feedback. This does not mean saying three positive comments and one negative comment when giving feedback to someone. It is good practice to remember to provide positive feedback to people whenever you can. That way, when you do need to give negative feedback, the feedback recipient will be more open to it, and will remember that you provide both positive and negative feedback.

Some tips about receiving feedback

Receiving feedback can be equally challenging. Although we may not admit it, most of us do not like to hear negative feedback.

1. Explicitly invite feedback
   - To demonstrate your openness to feedback, it is necessary for the coach to explicitly request feedback at the end of coaching conversations.
   - For example, "Now that we have come to the end of the coaching conversation, I wonder if you would be willing to give me some feedback about my performance as a coach? I am keen to have any feedback from you, positive or negative, so that I can improve my practice as a coach."

2. Listen actively to feedback that is provided
   - When the coachee starts to give you feedback, avoid the tendency to get defensive. Remain attentive and do your best listening. You should show your openness to feedback by maintaining open body language and nodding.
   - For example:
     Coachee: Well, you did actually make me feel uncomfortable at times. I don't know, it just felt awkward when you didn't say anything.

Coach: Ah, OK. So that felt awkward for you?

Coachee: Yes. Just once or twice. It's not a big deal, but I thought I would mention it.

Coach: Thank you for raising it. It's really helpful to have honest feedback.

3. Thank the provider of the feedback
   - As in the example above, remember to always thank anyone who gives you feedback. This shows that you are genuine about your desire for feedback and it will make it easier for this person to give you honest feedback again in the future.

4. Find time to consider the feedback before deciding whether to accept or reject it
   - Once you have heard the feedback and thanked the feedback provider, there is still a very important stage. This should be done in a quiet environment where it is possible to reflect on the feedback provided. Listening to feedback should not imply that people should accept whatever they are told. On the contrary, listening to the feedback is only the first step. It is an important step because many people reject feedback even before they consider it. In a quiet, reflective place the feedback recipient should consider whether the feedback is accurate or inaccurate. If it is accurate, then the feedback recipient can consider whether he or she wants to (a) start making some changes, (b) think about it further, or (c) seek further information. If the feedback recipient judges the information to be inaccurate, he or she can (a) simply reject the feedback, (b) reflect on the nature of the relationship between the feedback provider and feedback recipient, or (c) seek further information from the feedback provider.

Feedback is essential for development and growth, so it should be a part of our coaching conversations. Those who seek to improve need to become skilled at receiving and considering feedback. Those who seek to help others to improve need to become skilled at giving feedback.

At this point, we have covered the key skills of coaching: listening with purpose, asking powerful questions, paraphrasing, summarising, and giving and receiving feedback. As suggested in the introduction to this book, we believe that there are three elements to successful coaching: the skills of coaching, a coaching process, and a way of being. In the next chapters we will consider the coaching process and the way of being.

CHAPTER SEVEN

Ershad coaching framework

One of the responsibilities of a coach is to manage the coaching conversation in order to support the coachee towards a change in thinking or behaviour. Therefore, knowledge of a coaching process to use when working with a coachee is essential. While there are a number of coaching processes already in use in Western countries, we will propose below a new conversational framework for coaching in Islamic culture.

A typical coaching conversation

A typical coaching conversation takes place between two people (a coach and a coachee) in a suitable location. Normally, coaching conversations last between thirty minutes and two hours. It is common practice for the number and duration of coaching sessions to be agreed at the outset. As we have discussed already, the role of the coach is to listen, ask questions, summarise, and paraphrase appropriately. Coaches also have the responsibility for managing the conversational process so that the time available is used most effectively. This requires the coach to be familiar with a conversational process (such as the one presented in this chapter). The coach would then manage the conversation so that sufficient time is spent at the various stages. This allows the coachee to focus on the topic at hand and speak openly about what he or she wishes to achieve while the coach ensures that the conversation follows a process that will lead to some kind of change.

Contracting

Before coaching takes place, it is good practice for the coach and the coachee to enter into a formal agreement about the coaching relationship. Coaching conversations are professional conversations, so there is usually a brief contracting agreement before the coaching starts. During the contracting, the coach and the coachee will discuss the importance of confidentiality and its limits, agree the number of times they will meet, decide on the length of the coaching conversations, and make sure that both parties are aware of their responsibilities and roles. During this conversation, it is important to check that the coach and the coachee have the same understanding about what coaching is and each person's responsibilities. Contracting should precede the coaching framework covered in this chapter.

We will start by reviewing the reasons for developing a new conversational framework that we have called "Ershad coaching". First, we will remind ourselves of the purpose of the human race according to Islam. Once this has been reviewed, we will present an integrated coaching framework that supports this purpose. The framework incorporates some partnership conditions, the Ershad coaching process, and an alignment wheel.

The purpose of human beings

The key purpose for which God has created the human race is to worship Him through building, constructing, and cultivating life on earth. In Arabic, the word that captures the concept of "building, constructing, and cultivating life" is *e'maar*. We will use this word from here onwards. This concept provides the rationale for the development of the Ershad coaching framework. We hope that Ershad coaching will support people to engage actively with their duties of worship and *e'maar*.

The worshipping of God

God says in the Noble Qu'ran: "I have not created jinn and mankind except to serve Me" (51:56).

وَمَا خَلَقْتُ الْجِنَّ وَالْإِنسَ إِلَّا لِيَعْبُدُونِ - 51:56

This quote is explicit about the purpose of mankind. In the passage, the word "serve" can be understood as worship, incorporating the concepts of humility and submission towards God. The most general meaning of worship in Islam is inclusive of everything that is pleasing to God. This includes issues of belief or deeds of the body. It may include everything a person perceives, thinks, intends, feels, says, and does. It also refers to everything that God requires, including rituals as well as beliefs, work, social activities, and personal behaviour.

Another perspective regarding comprehensive acts of worship in Islam is presented by Dr Kilani's account of three aspects of worship: religious, social, and universal (Al-Kayali, 2008). The "religious aspect" refers to practising religious rites. The "social aspect" refers to having an honourable character and maintaining good relationships with others. The "universal aspect" refers to the precepts of a person in understanding and managing his or her relationship with the universe. This last aspect requires in-depth, insightful, and studious knowledge of the visible and invisible realms that we live in. A person's understanding of his or her position in the universe must encompass and integrate all three aspects as a prerequisite for him or her to see the "big picture". This allows people to fulfil their mission and purpose for being on earth.

E'maar

The second purpose of the creation of humans is to cultivate life on earth. God says in the Noble Qur'an: "And to Thamood their brother Salih; he said, 'O my people, serve God! You have no god other than He. It is He who produced you from the earth and has given you to live therein; so ask forgiveness of Him, then repent to Him; surely my Lord is nigh, and answers prayer" (11:61).

وَإِلَىٰ ثَمُودَ أَخَاهُمْ صَالِحًا ۚ قَالَ يَا قَوْمِ اعْبُدُوا اللَّهَ مَا لَكُم مِّنْ إِلَٰهٍ غَيْرُهُ ۖ هُوَ أَنشَأَكُم مِّنَ الْأَرْضِ
وَاسْتَعْمَرَكُمْ فِيهَا فَاسْتَغْفِرُوهُ ثُمَّ تُوبُوا إِلَيْهِ ۚ إِنَّ رَبِّي قَرِيبٌ مُّجِيبٌ - 11:61

E'maar or "making civilisation" can be understood as cultivating life on earth. This requires the human race to work hard. It also means that people should learn as much as they can. This involves the scientific methodology of observation, analysis, and conclusion. When this is managed well, people will be able to use their enhanced learning and scientific understanding for industrious purposes such as *e'maar*. If successful in this task, this will ensure that human beings can strive for perfection on this earth by serving their own species and all other species. In this way, people will be achieving their mission on earth.

The Noble Qur'an is a comprehensive text, providing guidance to human beings on how to build, prosper, and progress on earth. It teaches that people should develop good knowledge of life sciences by seeking and pursuing recent theories and discoveries in order to update scientific knowledge and continually refine their understanding. It is therefore imperative for anyone who is interested in achieving the divine purpose of *e'maar* to keep pace with change and innovation.

Abu Hamid al-Ghazali and his theory of science

Abu Hamid al-Ghazali was one of the pioneering scholars, writers, and researchers of science and culture (1051–1111 CE). In his writings, he explored the relationship of science, religion, and the world around us. These writings continue to influence the way we think about the role of science in Islam.

For a person to take part in civilisation, he or she must have a clear idea about the Creator of the universe and of this life. The Noble Qur'an links *e'maar* with taking the advice, counsel, and guidance of the prophets, peace be upon them. Whoever seeks to act while ignoring such heavenly guidance shall bring misery and war, and the fall of civilisation. As the Noble Qur'an states: "God has struck a similitude: a city that was secure, at rest, its provision coming to it easefully from every place, then it was unthankful for the blessings of God; so God let it taste the garment of hunger and of fear, for the things that they were working" (16:112).

وَضَرَبَ اللهُ مَثَلًا قَرْيَةً كَانَتْ آمِنَةً مُّطْمَئِنَّةً يَأْتِيهَا رِزْقُهَا رَغَدًا مِّن كُلِّ مَكَانٍ فَكَفَرَتْ بِأَنْعُمِ اللهِ فَأَذَاقَهَا اللهُ لِبَاسَ الْجُوعِ وَالْخَوْفِ بِمَا كَانُوا يَصْنَعُونَ - 16:112

Many of the stories of the Noble Qur'an reveal how advanced nations and civilisations expanded when they followed divine guidance and how they were plagued with corruption, conceit, and the fall of civilisation when they ignored the law of God.

An integrated coaching model

In light of the importance of people worshipping God and participating in *e'maar*, and our discussions in previous chapters about the history of coaching in the West (Chapter One) and the characteristics of Islamic culture (Chapter Two), we propose below a revised coaching framework that is more aligned with the values and principles of Islam.

Our system of Ershad coaching is a comprehensive framework that incorporates some partnership conditions, a conversational process, and the concept of an alignment wheel. The partnership conditions and the Ershad coaching process are covered in this chapter. The Alignment Wheel is discussed in detail in Chapter Eight. We believe that Ershad coaching will support powerful learning conversations that allow people to raise their self-awareness and understanding while encouraging them to take personal responsibility for working towards the right path.

As with existing coaching approaches, the coach's role (we will use the term "facilitator" from now on in relation to Ershad coaching) is to manage the conversational process by guiding the coachee (we will use the term "learner" from now on in relation to Ershad coaching) through a number of distinct phases. The facilitator should act as a partner to the learner, ensuring that the learner is thinking deeply and making appropriate decisions for him- or herself.

Ershad coaching framework

As shown on the next page, the outer ring of the Ershad coaching framework is called the "partnership conditions". This refers to the need for respectful and trusting relationships before the real work of Ershad coaching can begin. The partnership conditions can sustain ongoing, positive, and thoughtful relationships between the facilitator and the learner.

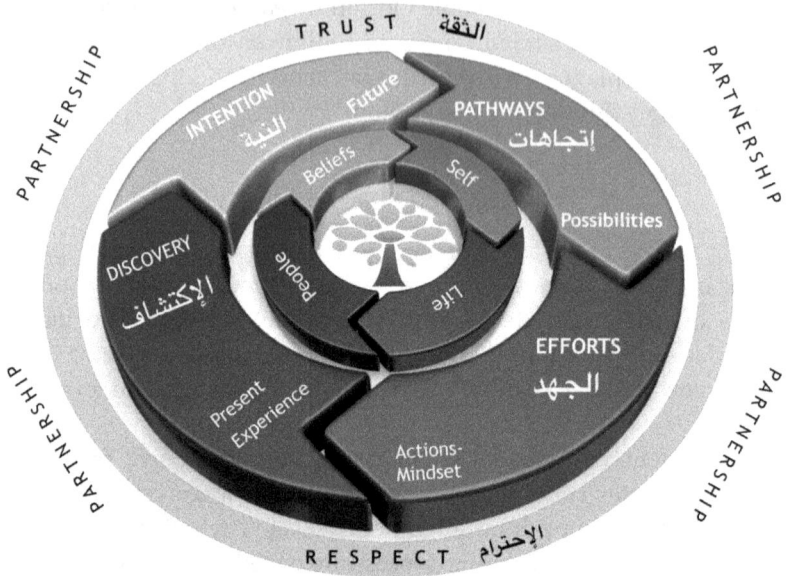

Figure 7.1. Ershad coaching framework.

Partnership conditions

Encompassing the Ershad coaching conversation are the partnership conditions necessary for effective relationships that can lead to sustained changes in behaviour and thinking. The partnership conditions should be discussed at the start of every Ershad coaching relationship. How will the two parties work together effectively? How can trust and respect be demonstrated within the coaching sessions? As part of this pre-coaching conversation, the broad topic is agreed upon and the length of the coaching relationship is discussed. Once both parties are comfortable with their respective roles (i.e., the facilitator as a conversational guide and thinking partner; the learner as the lead thinker and decision maker), the length of time allocated to the upcoming conversation should be agreed. This pre-coaching conversation should feel like a dialogue between equals who are deciding the best way to have a productive conversation. While both are of equal status, it is to be remembered that the focus of the conversation is always the development of the learner.

Facilitator:	Al-salaamu aleykum [peace be on you]
Learner:	Aleykum al-salaam [and upon you]
Facilitator:	How are you?
Learner:	Well, with thanks to God.
Facilitator:	How can I help you?
Learner:	I don't know if you can help me, but my friend advised me to come and see you. He told me that you are a coach and that you will be able to support me.
Facilitator:	Tell me more about what are you looking for.
Learner:	I am going through a big change in my life. I have just been promoted to a new managerial position in a new department in my company. Not only that, I am expecting a new baby within the next three months. I feel that I have a lot going on around me and I feel stuck. I don't know how you can help me.
Facilitator:	What do you know about coaching?
Learner:	Not much. I think you are an experienced consultant who is able to support clients in different fields.
Facilitator:	Not exactly, although I am here to support you. A coach is a partner who will work with you in professional and personal areas that require development based on your own needs.
Learner:	Great, how can we start?
Facilitator:	Tell me first, when do you want to start the coaching?
Learner:	Next week.
Facilitator:	How often would you like us to meet?
Learner:	How about twice a month? Is this possible?
Facilitator:	Sure. Why not? During coaching sessions, I will listen to you, ask questions to motivate you and I will challenge your answers and ideas. How does that sound to you?
Learner:	I am looking forward to it.
Facilitator:	Any concerns or needs you want me to consider during our coaching relationship?
Learner:	Not at the moment.
Facilitator:	Great. Please also note that we as coaches honour confidentiality in our relationship with our clients.
Learner:	This is very important to me.
Facilitator:	Is next Monday a good day to start?
Learner:	Yes.
Facilitator:	I will send the agreement for six months. Please review and sign the agreement. I will also send additional information about coaching for you to read.

Facilitator's role in building the partnership conditions

The main responsibility for building the partnership conditions lies with the facilitator. We see the partnership conditions as foundational. Only when these conditions are experienced by the learner is it likely that a strong professional relationship can be developed. First, the facilitator should be trustworthy. This means that the facilitator is able to maintain strict confidentiality, ensuring that what is discussed in Ershad coaching conversations remains "in the room". The learner may discuss what transpires during the conversation, but the facilitator must not share this information with others. Being trustworthy includes keeping any promises and staying within the coaching agreement. Second, the facilitator should adopt a non-judgmental attitude. The facilitator should not form judgments over the learner regardless of what he or she says. Rather, it is the opposite. The facilitator should accept whatever the learner says with an open and curious mind. The facilitator's role in Ershad coaching is to support the learner, not to evaluate him or her. Third, the facilitator should be positive and future-focused. This means that, in general terms, the facilitator is more attentive to the learner's strengths, resources, and capabilities. The facilitator should turn the attention of the conversation to a positive future and maintain a focus on the learner's intention. Finally, the facilitator should be at all times respectful of the learner. This includes all facets of treating a person with deserved respect but also includes respecting the learner's right to make his or her own decisions. As a thinking partner, the facilitator should create a thoughtful environment but should not do the thinking for the learner.

In addition to the important role of developing and maintaining the partnership conditions, the facilitator is also responsible for managing the conversational process, which will be explained below. As the facilitator manages the process, he or she will need to employ the coaching skills of listening with purpose (see Chapter Three), asking powerful questions (see Chapter Four), summarising and paraphrasing (see Chapter Five), and providing feedback (see Chapter Six). So the facilitator needs to carry the responsibility of building the partnership conditions and managing a conversational process. The learner also has responsibilities. The first is to take personal responsibility for his or her own development and progress. The second is to contribute to the partnership conditions.

Learner's role in building the partnership conditions

Having underscored the importance of the facilitator's responsibility in this regard, it should be noted that the learner also has a significant role in influencing the conditions that are discussed here. The learner has more choices about his or her attitude towards the coaching and his or her engagement overall. However, to achieve successful outcomes it would be expected that the learner is willing to be open to new ideas. A readiness to engage fully with the Ershad coaching framework is important. He or she should also be prepared to share honest feelings and thoughts about the current situation and his or her intention for the future. It will also be in the learner's best interests to attempt to implement any new ideas or behaviours in-between coaching sessions. These respective roles in developing the partnership conditions should be discussed in the initial stages. Clarity about the partnership will increase the likelihood of effective coaching conversations.

Respect in Islam

Respect is a value that is central to human beings and should be expressed towards everything around them. In other words, people should engage with what is around them respectfully, carefully, and with commitment. The Ershad coaching framework provides an opportunity for learners to think about their relationship with others and their environment.

Islam has given respect a great focus and it extends to most of the relationships that bind Muslims with others. A Muslim is ordered to respect other Muslims and non-Muslims alike. The Prophet, peace be upon him, was a role model of this when he wrote to the Roman King of Egypt at the time: "In the name of God the Merciful, Muhammad is the messenger of God, to the great Roman King ..." (Sahih Muslim, Book 32, Hadith 89). The Prophet, peace be upon him, did not curse him, nor did he threaten to harm him, but addressed him with respect.

Islam has emphasised the value of respect and linked it to the actions and behaviours that ensure achievable religious obedience (worship) to God. It is not an abstract moral value but one that is humanly accessible and will ultimately be rewarded. Respect, as pictured in Islam, is varied and encompasses other values such as self-esteem, respect for parents, women, society, the elderly, scientists, leaders, and non-Muslims.

1. Self-esteem
Self-esteem is the mental image a person draws of him- or herself. This image is formed by the person's experience and circumstances and is strongly influenced by the messages that are received from others. Without a doubt, the way people see themselves has a strong effect on all aspects of their lives.

2. Respect for parents
One should respect parents by honouring and revering them. God has linked proper worship to the kindness shown to parents: "Thy Lord has decreed you shall not serve any but Him, and to be good to parents, whether one or both of them attains old age with thee; say not to them 'Fie', neither chide them, but speak unto them words respectful" (17:23).

وَقَضَىٰ رَبُّكَ أَلَّا تَعْبُدُوا إِلَّا إِيَّاهُ وَبِالْوَالِدَيْنِ إِحْسَانًا ۚ إِمَّا يَبْلُغَنَّ عِندَكَ الْكِبَرَ أَحَدُهُمَا أَوْ كِلَاهُمَا فَلَا تَقُل لَّهُمَا أُفٍّ وَلَا تَنْهَرْهُمَا وَقُل لَّهُمَا قَوْلًا كَرِيمًا - 17:23

3. Respect for women
God sent the Prophet, peace be upon him, at a time when most nations denied the humanity of women. Arabs, before Islam, regarded women as a commodity, or a sub-creature whose purpose was to serve men. Islam honoured women stressing the necessity of showing respect to them, and made woman equal to man with shared duties, responsibilities, and rights. Man and woman were considered two branches of the same tree. The Prophet, peace be upon him, said: "Know that a woman is the twin half of a man" (narrated by Aisha, Ummul Mu'minin: Sunan Abi Dawud, Book 1, Hadith 236).

"O mankind, We have created you male and female, and appointed you races and tribes, that you may know one another. Surely the noblest among you in the sight of God is the most godfearing of you. God is All-knowing, All-aware" (Noble Qur'an, 49:13).

يَا أَيُّهَا النَّاسُ إِنَّا خَلَقْنَاكُم مِّن ذَكَرٍ وَأُنثَىٰ وَجَعَلْنَاكُمْ شُعُوبًا وَقَبَائِلَ لِتَعَارَفُوا ۚ إِنَّ أَكْرَمَكُمْ عِندَ اللَّهِ أَتْقَاكُمْ ۚ إِنَّ اللَّهَ عَلِيمٌ خَبِيرٌ - 49:13

Men and women, in Islam, are equal in duties and responsibilities. They both face equal penalties and individual freedoms. Humanity is only as strong and may only progress with the stable and strong standing of both men and women where women are expected to respect men and vice versa.

4. Respect for the young and the old

   In Islam, it is important to respect and appreciate the young, giving them a sense of dignity and self-confidence as this builds their minds and enhances their self-worth, giving them a sense of purpose. Sahl ibn Saad, may God be pleased with him, reported that the Messenger of God (peace be upon him) was served a drink and drank from it first. A young child sat on his right and an old man was on his left. He asked the young boy, "Would you allow me to serve the people on my left first?" The boy said, "No, it's my turn" (not wanting to give away the privilege of drinking after the Prophet, peace be upon him). The Prophet then turned back to the child and put the drink in his hand (Al-Bukhari and Muslim—Book 1, Hadith 569).

   Muslims are also commanded to respect the elderly. As narrated by Abdullah ibn Amr ibn al-'As, the Prophet (peace be upon him) said: "Those who do not show mercy to our young ones and do not realise the right of our elders are not from us" (Sunan Abu Dawud, Book 42, Hadith 4925). It is neither ethical nor moral if one fails to show elders respect and appreciation.

5. Respect for scholars and scientists

   God has raised believers and scholars. According to him, "God will raise up in rank those of you who believe and have been given knowledge. And God is aware of the things you do" (58:11). Respect for scientists and their work (Fatawi) is to respect the legacy of the prophets. Scholars are the heirs of the prophets and they have their status and virtue.

يَا أَيُّهَا الَّذِينَ آمَنُوا إِذَا قِيلَ لَكُمْ تَفَسَّحُوا فِي الْمَجَالِسِ فَافْسَحُوا يَفْسَحِ اللَّهُ لَكُمْ ۖ وَإِذَا قِيلَ انشُزُوا فَانشُزُوا يَرْفَعِ اللَّهُ الَّذِينَ آمَنُوا مِنكُمْ وَالَّذِينَ أُوتُوا الْعِلْمَ دَرَجَاتٍ ۚ وَاللَّهُ بِمَا تَعْمَلُونَ خَبِيرٌ - 58:11

6. Respect for leaders

   The Noble Qur'an commands that people should respect and obey their leaders. God says: "O believers, obey God, and obey the Messenger and those in authority among you" (4:59).

يَا أَيُّهَا الَّذِينَ آمَنُوا أَطِيعُوا اللَّهَ وَأَطِيعُوا الرَّسُولَ وَأُولِي الْأَمْرِ مِنكُمْ ۖ فَإِن تَنَازَعْتُمْ فِي شَيْءٍ فَرُدُّوهُ إِلَى اللَّهِ وَالرَّسُولِ إِن كُنتُمْ تُؤْمِنُونَ بِاللَّهِ وَالْيَوْمِ الْآخِرِ ۚ ذَٰلِكَ خَيْرٌ وَأَحْسَنُ تَأْوِيلًا - 4:59

7. Respect for non-Muslims

   Islamic law is not limited to ensuring respect between Muslims. It necessitates respect for Muslims and non-Muslims, in various ways, including respect for human dignity, compassion, and fairness. According to the Noble Qur'an, "Dispute not with the People of the Book save in the fairer manner, except for those of them that do wrong; and say, 'We believe in what has been sent down to us, and what has been sent down to you; our God and your God is One, and to Him we have surrendered'" (29:46).

وَلَا تُجَادِلُوا أَهْلَ الْكِتَابِ إِلَّا بِالَّتِي هِيَ أَحْسَنُ إِلَّا الَّذِينَ ظَلَمُوا مِنْهُمْ وَقُولُوا آمَنَّا بِالَّذِي أُنزِلَ إِلَيْنَا وَأُنزِلَ
إِلَيْكُمْ وَإِلَهُنَا وَإِلَهُكُمْ وَاحِدٌ وَنَحْنُ لَهُ مُسْلِمُونَ - 29:46

Ershad coaching conversation

Having discussed the partnership conditions, the facilitator and learner should be ready to undertake the coaching conversation. They will have explored how best to work together and will have an idea of the broad topic that will form the basis of the coaching interactions. Within the Ershad coaching framework, the conversational process incorporates the following phases: discovery, intention, pathways, and effort. Each of these will be discussed below.

Discovery

To understand the context of the learner and to start to build a strong relationship, the facilitator begins by listening actively during the discovery phase. Together, the facilitator and the learner should do their best to understand the current situation in relation to the topic for the conversation. While it may be helpful to understand both the experiences as well as the present situation, weight should be given to the *current* situation. The facilitator's role is to support the learner to see the current situation from a number of different perspectives. An important aspect of this phase is to build up the confidence of the learner and to identify existing resources and strengths that can be used as a foundation for his or her future achievements. The purpose of this stage is an increase in self-awareness by creating thinking time for the learner. The facilitator should decide how much time should be spent in this phase. Early in the

Ershad coaching relationship (first and second coaching conversations), it is likely that relatively more time will be required as the learner reflects on his or her experiences. The establishment of "This is who I am" by the learner is an important outcome of this part of the framework.

The facilitator can ask questions such as:

"In relation to your topic, what is happening at the moment?"
"Tell me about yourself in relation to the topic of our conversation."
"How would you describe the current situation?"
"What strengths do you already have to pursue your intention?"
"What is good about what is happening now?"
"What are the factors getting in the way of your success?"
"Who else is involved in this situation?"
"What's motivating you to think about this at this time?"
"How do you feel about what is happening?"
"What are your thoughts about what is happening?"
"What do others think about this situation?"
"What are the most significant factors for you at the moment?"

Facilitator: Salam! How are you?
Learner: Salam. I am fine, thank you.
Facilitator: How do you want to spend our time today?
Learner: I want to discuss some personal issues for which I need some clarification.
Facilitator: What exactly are you looking for when you say "personal issues"?
Learner: I am not satisfied or comfortable with some of my achievements in life.
Facilitator: Please tell me what is going on in your life right now.
Learner: I have been working as a marketing manager for seven years, working from 9 am–9 pm, six days a week. I have two children, a five-year-old and a seven-year-old. I love my wife but I feel that I am not doing enough for my family but also not getting what I want from my work.
Facilitator: What do you want from your life and work?
Learner: I want to be happy, enjoying my life with my wife and children. And at work I want to be a successful leader.

Facilitator:	As we have only one hour for our session today, what do you want to focus on?
Learner:	I guess my work—my career.
Facilitator:	What are you looking for?
Learner:	I want to be promoted to VP in marketing. I have the experience and knowledge and I believe that I deserve to be in this position.
Facilitator:	What is appealing to you about this position?
Learner:	It's the next level, and I have always wanted to be a VP.
Facilitator:	What is your intention behind this?

Intention

The discovery phase is followed by the intention phase. Intention has great stature in Islam. It is at the heart of how people will be judged by God and it underpins both worship and *e'maar*. Identifying the correct intention therefore becomes crucial. This means that any actions intended to respond to God's teaching will be accepted and rewarded. Intention can be understood as a compass for directing, navigating, and adjusting human behaviour.

It has been narrated on the authority of Omar bin al Khattab, may God be pleased with him, that he heard the Prophet, peace be upon him, saying: "(the value of) an action depends on the intention behind it. A man will be rewarded only for what he intended. The emigration of one who emigrates for the sake of God and his Messenger is for the sake of God and his Messenger; and one who emigrates for gaining a worldly advantage or for marrying a woman is for what he has emigrated." (Al-Bukhari & Muslim—Book 1, Hadith 1).

The Hadith above shows that a person is judged on his or her intention. So if a person's journey is to seek God and His Prophet, then he or she will be judged and rewarded accordingly. Conversely, if a person's journey in life is to seek material gains, or to be physically with a woman or to have worldly riches then that was his intention and this is what he will be judged for" (Sahih Muslim—Book 33, Hadith 222).

We can consider a person's actions through two aspects: the intangible and the tangible. The intangible relates to a person's plans, goals, reasons, or motivations. All of this can be understood as a person's intention. On the other hand, the tangible aspect comprises the actions themselves—the materialising of the intention in the living world. From an Islamic point of view, it is the intangible (the intention) that is the part that is rewarded or punished. To understand intention, it is therefore helpful at times for the coach to ask the "why" question (see box below).

> Earlier in this book, we have advised against using the "why" question because it can trigger defensiveness in the learner. We argued that such questions could seem "investigative". However, in the intention phase, we actively support the learner to be aware of the alignment between what he or she wants to achieve and his or her intentions. For this reason, the "why" question is an important part of the intention phase.

Ibn Abbas, may God be pleased with him, said that the Prophet, peace be upon him, said that God would judge a man or a woman for their intentions. If a person has good intentions but does not follow through on them, he or she would be rewarded; but if a person does follow through on the good intention, he or she would get multiple rewards. Conversely, if a person has bad intentions and does not act on them, he or she would also be rewarded. However, if a person acts on the bad intentions, he or she shall be judged equally to the weight of that sin (Al-Bukhari and Muslim: Book 1, Hadith 11).

The intention phase is therefore a very important part of Ershad coaching. A learner should consider his or her intentions at an early point in the conversation. In the life of a Muslim any work undertaken or intended to be achieved must be consistent with his beliefs and that takes into account this life and the hereafter.

> ### Sincerity is required for prosperity and success
>
> Intention is a legitimate concept that entails working faithfully for the sake of God alone: "They were commanded only to serve God, making the religion His sincerely, men of pure faith, and to perform the prayer, and pay the alms" (Noble Qu'ran, 98:5).
>
> وَمَا أُمِرُوا إِلَّا لِيَعْبُدُوا اللَّهَ مُخْلِصِينَ لَهُ الدِّينَ حُنَفَاءَ وَيُقِيمُوا الصَّلَاةَ وَيُؤْتُوا الزَّكَاةَ ۚ وَذَٰلِكَ دِينُ الْقَيِّمَةِ -
>
> 98:5

Sincerity

- Asking God to witness your work
- Devotion and sincerity is a way of filtering one's actions
- It is important that there is alignment between intention and behaviour.

Benefits of sincerity

- Enlightenment
- Spiritual strength
- Perseverance.

This means that for Muslims, having the correct intention and behaving accordingly can be considered a form of worship that brings benefits in a person's life and rewards in the hereafter.

In this phase, the learner should attempt to identify his or her aspirations or intention for the future. In other words, the learner should articulate what he or she hopes to achieve. As a result, there should be a clear future focus during this part of the conversation. The facilitator's role is to help the learner articulate and understand his or her intention for the future. What is the reason that the learner wishes to achieve the intention that he or she has set? To be clear about what the learner wants in the future *and* for the learner to understand the true intention behind this desire is the purpose of this stage. In Ershad coaching, it is essential that the intention is a positive one, and sometimes it may be necessary for the facilitator to help the learner to reconsider his or her intention.

At this point in the conversation, therefore, the learner should have a better understanding of his or her current situation and resources (*discovery phase*) and his or her intention for the future with his or her reasons for wanting this (*intention phase*). The gap between where the learner is now and where he or she wishes to be should be discussed before proceeding to the pathways phase. Does the learner believe that he or she has set an achievable intention?

God created people of different physical and mental abilities, intended to be used in accordance with their personal needs and the surrounding environment. People who are aware of their potential will be able

The facilitator can ask questions such as:

"What do you want to achieve?"
"What does your desired future look like?"
"How will you know that you have achieved what you want?"
"What is important to you about this?"
"What makes these aspirations worth fighting for?"
"Tell me about what you want for yourself and those around you."
"What is the target that you want to work towards?"
"What are your aspirations?"
"What could you achieve if you put your mind to it?"
"What is your intention behind doing this?"

Facilitator:	What are you looking for?
Learner:	I want to learn how to be a great leader.
Facilitator:	Tell me, what does the word "leader" mean to you?
Learner:	A leader inspires people, supports them to reach the organisation's goals, and takes risks.
Facilitator:	What else?
Learner:	The leader takes decisions and has an impact on organisational progress.
Facilitator:	Why is this important to you?
Learner:	It's very important.
Facilitator:	Tell me more about it.
Learner:	This is a good question—Why it is important to me? (Moment of silence.) I want my children and family to be proud of me.
Facilitator:	What else?
Learner:	People will respect me more.
Facilitator:	What is the relation between leadership and respect?
Learner:	The *leader* should be respectful.
Facilitator:	And what is your *intention* behind wanting to be a respectful leader?

to exploit their abilities to pursue their mission in this life. God says, "Surely your striving is to diverse ends" (92:4).

إِنَّ سَعْيَكُمْ لَشَتَّىٰ - 92:4

This means that the actions of His servants are varied. There are those who will do good and there are those who will do evil.

I said, "O God's Messenger (peace be upon him)! Why should people try to do good deeds?" The Prophet (peace be upon him) said, "Everybody will find easy to do such deeds as will lead him to his destined place for which he has been created" (narrated by Imran).

Sahih al-Bukhari: Book 97, Hadith 176

Things to consider when identifying an intention:

- Is it too easily achievable? If so, this may need to be reconsidered. It is possible that the learner will not be as motivated by a seemingly insignificant step.
- Is it too much of a leap from where the learner is now to the intention for the future? If so, the learner may wish to identify an interim stage. It is important for coaching that the learner feels that he or she is making progress towards his or her intention.
- Does the learner seem motivated by this? If not, it may be helpful to explore the reasons for this.

Pathways

When there is clarity about the learner's current situation and intention, it is time to start exploring different ways of moving forward. The pathways stage involves the learner identifying a number of possible pathways or routes from the current position towards the intention. It should be recognised that a number of different routes may exist, and these are to be explored during this phase. To facilitate the type of creative thinking required, the learner should be encouraged to generate as many pathways as possible. Initially, it is helpful to invite the learner to think broadly, generating as many ideas as he or she can. The Alignment Wheel (which will be discussed in Chapter Eight) will be used to check that the pathways are aligned with the learner's beliefs and environment at a later stage.

The facilitator can ask questions such as:

"What pathways can you see?"
"Can you think of a route that will take you from where you are now towards your intention?"
"How can you start to work towards your desired future?"
"What options are available?"
"What is the thinking needed to move you forward?"
"What possibilities emerge when you think about this?"
"Tell me of options that you have already considered."
"What has to happen now so that you are more likely to move towards your intention?"
"As you think carefully about this, what options come to mind?"
"Can you identify the most direct path to what you want to achieve?"

Facilitator:	Where are you now?
Learner:	I know what it means to be a leader. But why do I want to become a leader? I'm not sure. And what are the specifications of a leader?
Facilitator:	Where are you now as a leader, on a scale of 0 as low and 10 as high?
Learner:	I would say that I am currently at 5.
Facilitator:	What makes it a 5, rather than a 0?
Learner:	Well, as I mentioned, I think I have a good idea of what it means to be a leader. I have also held a number of management positions in this company. So my experience of management is important. Finally, it is a 5 because I feel that I have the inclination to be a leader.
Facilitator:	And where do you want to be in a year's time?
Learner:	Perhaps a 7?
Facilitator:	What do you need to do to reach 7, in your opinion?
Learner:	I need to develop myself in different areas.
Facilitator:	What do you mean by different areas?
Learner:	I mean leadership skills, communication, performance ...
Facilitator:	OK. So let us now consider ways in which we can improve your outcomes in some of these areas.

Coaching will work best when there is full engagement from the learner and he or she is fully participating in the generation of ideas and pathways. For this reason, a number of different approaches to this ideal are recommended. It is helpful to remember that most of the coaching conversation is simply a discussion between two people. This phase should feel energetic and purposeful. At the very least, the learner should be writing down the pathways that are generated. It may be helpful to ask the learner to undertake some activities to encourage him or her to think in new ways.

Activities:

Ask the learner to write out his or her pathways on post-it notes.
Ask the learner to draw the various possibilities.
Ask the learner to create a mind map of the options.
Ask the learner to imagine that he or she is advising someone else about the same situation.

Once the possibilities have been explored, an important aspect of this process is the assessment of the pathways through the use of the Alignment Wheel (see Chapter Eight). Each of the pathways should be considered in relation to ethics, values, and beliefs that are important to the learner. This process is managed by the facilitator who should adopt a non-judgmental, non-directive approach.

When each pathway has been checked against the Alignment Wheel, it is the learner's task to select the one that he or she believes will be the most helpful in the next step. At this stage, the facilitator should verify that the selected pathway will bring the learner closer to his or her intention as identified earlier in the Ershad coaching process.

Effort

The final phase of the coaching conversation is arguably the most important as it relates to the determination to think and behave differently in order to move towards the learner's intention. The subphases (behaviour and mindset) are significant in this endeavour. The learner should identify the new thinking (mindset) that will be needed in order to implement the adapted behaviour between coaching sessions. The extent to which the learner will need to focus on one or other of the subphases will vary. In many cases both will be of equal weighting.

The facilitator can ask questions such as:

"What new ways of thinking are required?"

"What will you do differently as a result of this conversation?"

"How will you start to implement what we have discussed?"

"What is your plan of action?"

"What will you have achieved by the next time we meet?"

"Could you summarise to me what you will do next?"

"How will you put this into practice?"

"What is going to change as a result of this conversation?"

"How will you monitor your progress?"

"What will tell you that you have moved closer to your intention?"

"How will you know that you are being successful with this course of action?"

Facilitator: Could you summarise what options or pathways you think will help you to be a great leader?

Learner: One option is to attend a leadership skills training programme.

Facilitator: Anything else?

Learner: Search for, buy, and read books about leadership.

Facilitator: OK. What else?

Learner: Also ask for performance and personal feedback from my peers and my direct manager.

Facilitator: Having considered these options, what is your plan of action?

Learner: I think I should contact the career development department to attend the next leadership training programme. I will also contact my colleagues for their feedback. Can we discuss the feedback at our next coaching session?

Facilitator: Good idea. It sounds like you have some ideas about practical things you can do. Has this coaching session been helpful?

Learner: Yes. I want to thank you. It's been very helpful.

Facilitator: Thank you for the feedback. What was helpful to you?

Learner: I realised through talking to you that leadership is a way of being, not a position.

By the end of this phase, the learner should be clear about the thinking that is needed and the new behaviours that will be put into practice. The facilitator can assist by supporting the learner to be specific about the behaviours, the timescales, and the ways in which the changes will be measured.

In the final stages of the conversation, the facilitator should check whether the learner has achieved the outcome he or she wanted from the coaching conversation. This is also a good opportunity to solicit feedback about the coaching session. What worked well for the learner? How did he or she feel during the session? This information can be used to confirm a positive experience or improve future coaching conversations.

Conclusion

In this chapter we have presented the various stages of the Ershad coaching framework. We believe that this conversational process can be used to support others to make better decisions and enhance their learning and development in an authentic way. The learner's intentions and possible options should be checked for alignment so that his or her development takes place in a way that is congruent with his or her beliefs and values. This concept is discussed further in the next chapter.

CHAPTER EIGHT

The Alignment Wheel

In the previous chapter, we presented the partnership conditions and the conversational process of the Ershad coaching framework. This chapter will focus on the role of the Alignment Wheel, which is the third key component.

As we have stated, it is important for the learner to work towards an intention that is aligned with his or her beliefs and principles. Islam provides practical guidance about how Muslims should conduct their lives on earth. This guidance can support learners to make better decisions about intentions and behaviour. The essential mission of a Muslim is to "purify" him- or herself by means of acquiring appropriate knowledge of God and worshipping Him in the proper manner. At the same time, a person should strengthen human ties, ensuring that these are based on noble principles such as love, fraternity, equality, and fairness (Al-Zubeidi, 2008). From an Islamic perspective, the purpose of learning is for a person to attain the "best stature". This means being wholesome and complete, as is prescribed in the Noble Qur'an: "We indeed created Man in the fairest stature" (95:4).

لَقَدْ خَلَقْنَا الْإِنسَانَ فِي أَحْسَنِ تَقْوِيمٍ - 95:4

According to Ibn-Taymiyya, "In order for the human being to attain this rank of servitude to the Divine, he or she should have the intention, to say and do all that the Divine loves and accepts, of words and deeds, as reflected in the form of prayers, fasting, giving of alms, performing pilgrimage, speaking the truth, fulfilling obligations, honouring one's parents and kinship, keeping promises, encouraging good deeds and rebuffing wrongdoings, being good to one's neighbour, to orphans, the needy and to wayfarers and to do supplications, remembrance, and the reading of the Noble Qur'an, and such other noble forms of worshipping of the Divine" (quoted in Al-Zubeidi, 2008, p. 79).

Building of the complete and wholesome Muslim character requires continuous learning and development, and we believe that Ershad coaching can play an important part in this process. In other words, Ershad coaching can be used to support people to follow the "right path" and attain the "fairest stature".

The spiritual dimension

The actual meaning of the spiritual dimension in Islam is the relationship with God as well as the attachment of oneself in terms of faith and belief. This is at the heart of Muslim character. However, Islamic religion does not only focus on the concept of belief in God. Islam provides a complete and comprehensive educational methodology to support the process of progress and development in order to achieve its people's aspirations of happiness, success, peace, and tranquility.

The spiritual component is the essence of Islamic education. It has been established with solid foundations to consolidate the relationship between Muslims and God, linking life in this world with the hereafter. Moral education has closely accompanied Islamic education, supported by social education. The most important energy and power comes through mentioning the name of God and praising Him, reciting the Noble Qur'an, obeying and worshiping God, and praying to Him.

One of the most influential features in the spiritual education of Islam is the need for moderation and balance between the demands of body and soul. For example, worship should cover both aspects—the spiritual and the material. Worshipping practices are varied and repeated in order to keep Muslims spiritually pure and renewable, keeping them closer to God and His divine presence.

The advantages of moderation have been mentioned in many verses in the Noble Qur'an. In some of them, we find encouragement for believers to request both spiritual and materialistic outcomes as we have noted earlier: "But seek, amidst that which God has given thee, the Last Abode, and forget not thy portion of the present world; and do good, as God has been good to thee. And seek not to work corruption in the earth; surely God loves not the workers of corruption" (Noble Qur'an, 28:77).

وَابْتَغِ فِيمَا آتَاكَ اللهُ الدَّارَ الْآخِرَةَ وَلَا تَنسَ نَصِيبَكَ مِنَ الدُّنْيَا وَأَحْسِن كَمَا أَحْسَنَ اللهُ إِلَيْكَ وَلَا تَبْغِ الْفَسَادَ فِي الْأَرْضِ إِنَّ اللَّهَ لَا يُحِبُّ الْمُفْسِدِينَ - 28:77

In other verses in the Noble Qur'an, we find that God guides his believers to ask for a combination of life and afterlife requests, as seen below:

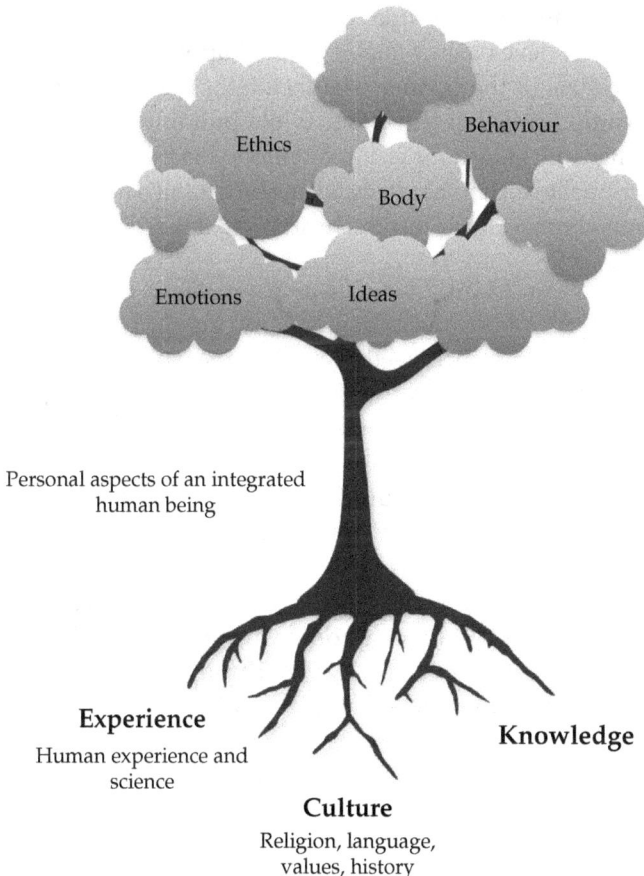

Ethics

Behaviour

Body

Emotions   Ideas

Personal aspects of an integrated
human being

Experience
Human experience and
science

Knowledge

Culture
Religion, language,
values, history

Figure 8.1. Human configuration.

"Now some men there are who say, 'Our Lord, give to us in this world'; such men shall have no part in the world to come. And others there are who say, 'Our Lord, give to us in this world good, and good in the world to come, and guard us against the chastisement of the fire'; those—they shall have a portion from what they have earned; and God is swift at the reckoning" (2:201–202).

وَمِنْهُم مَّن يَقُولُ رَبَّنَا آتِنَا فِي الدُّنْيَا حَسَنَةً وَفِي الْآخِرَةِ حَسَنَةً وَقِنَا عَذَابَ النَّارِ - 2:201
أُولَئِكَ لَهُمْ نَصِيبٌ مِّمَّا كَسَبُواْ ۚ وَاللهُ سَرِيعُ الْحِسَابِ - 2:202

Coaching and spirituality

The Ershad coaching facilitator should therefore focus on the mechanisms that enhance the spiritual dimension of the learner, supporting him or her to achieve balance, stability, and happiness based on the fundamental beliefs of the learner. The facilitator can help the learner to move towards his or her intentions while building on past successes and praising God. For example, it is mentioned in the Noble Qur'an that "Those who believe, their hearts being at rest in God's remembrance—in God's remembrance are at rest the hearts" (13:28).

الَّذِينَ آمَنُوا وَتَطْمَئِنُّ قُلُوبُهُم بِذِكْرِ اللهِ ۗ أَلَا بِذِكْرِ اللهِ تَطْمَئِنُّ الْقُلُوبُ - 13:28

For learners, this can be achieved by reading the Noble Qur'an, praising God, and saying prayers as mentioned by the Prophet Muhammad, peace be upon him. Doing this will allow the learner to do more good deeds, acts of worship, and continuous fruitful work. Mentioning God is, in itself, a heartfelt communication with God and is therefore a constructive spiritual activity. God says: "Then your hearts became hardened thereafter and are like stones, or even yet harder; for there are stones from which rivers come gushing, and others split, so that water issues from them, and others crash down in the fear of God. And God is not heedless of the things you do" (2:74). Through Ershad coaching, we can support learners to achieve "balance" or "alignment".

ثُمَّ قَسَتْ قُلُوبُكُم مِّن بَعْدِ ذَلِكَ فَهِيَ كَالْحِجَارَةِ أَوْ أَشَدُّ قَسْوَةً ۚ وَإِنَّ مِنَ الْحِجَارَةِ لَمَا يَتَفَجَّرُ مِنْهُ الْأَنْهَارُ ۚ
وَإِنَّ مِنْهَا لَمَا يَشَّقَّقُ فَيَخْرُجُ مِنْهُ الْمَاءُ ۚ وَإِنَّ مِنْهَا لَمَا يَهْبِطُ مِنْ خَشْيَةِ اللهِ ۗ وَمَا اللهُ بِغَافِلٍ عَمَّا تَعْمَلُونَ -
2:74

Alignment: balancing factors in Islam

Life is a series of processes based on elements such as compatibility and balancing. We understand this as "alignment". Alignment allows people to modify their behaviour in order to respond to different situations arising from human needs and desires. It is important that our responses are appropriate to specific situations and that they lead eventually to meeting one's own motives and needs through the use of one's capabilities. Alignment is therefore an individual's ability to adapt properly with his or her surroundings by achieving a balance within the environment in which he or she lives. This is a dynamic, ongoing process that should lead to increasingly harmonious relationships. Achieving this kind of alignment can lead to a feeling of balance and enhanced well-being. The ideal outcome of such alignment is what is termed the "assured self". Through Ershad coaching, it is possible to support people to work towards this.

The self in the Noble Qur'an

The self is the essence that distinguishes humans from all other creation, as it allows them to think and be conscious of what they see around them, to deliberate and make decisions, to pass judgments and understand the world, making choices to live as free, dignified agents. The self allows human beings to distinguish between right and wrong and to accept the consequences of choices that come with various behaviours, in this life and the hereafter. The characteristics of the human self are portrayed in the Noble Qur'an as follows:

1. The human self has limited energy. Therefore, as we have noted previously, it will not be assigned more tasks than it can handle: "God charges no soul save to its capacity" (2:286).

لَا يُكَلِّفُ اللهُ نَفْسًا إِلَّا وُسْعَهَا - 2:286

2. The self is a single soul. "Mankind, fear your Lord, who created you of a single soul" (4:1).

يَا أَيُّهَا النَّاسُ اتَّقُوا رَبَّكُمُ الَّذِي خَلَقَكُم مِّن نَّفْسٍ وَاحِدَةٍ - 4:1

3. The self is responsible for its actions, whether right or wrong: "Beware of a day when no soul for another shall give satisfaction, and no intercession shall be accepted from it, nor any counterpoise be taken, neither shall they be helped" (2:48).

وَاتَّقُوا يَوْمًا لَّا تَجْزِي نَفْسٌ عَن نَّفْسٍ شَيْئًا وَلَا يُقْبَلُ مِنْهَا شَفَاعَةٌ وَلَا يُؤْخَذُ مِنْهَا عَدْلٌ وَلَا هُمْ يُنصَرُونَ -
2:48

4. The self receives either reward or punishment according to its actions: "The day that every soul shall come disputing in its own behalf; and every soul shall be paid in full for what it wrought, and they shall not be wronged" (16:111).

يَوْمَ تَأْتِي كُلُّ نَفْسٍ تُجَادِلُ عَن نَّفْسِهَا وَتُوَفَّىٰ كُلُّ نَفْسٍ مَّا عَمِلَتْ وَهُمْ لَا يُظْلَمُونَ - 16:111

5. The self experiences regret and self-blame if it commits bad deeds, and a feeling of contentment and reassurance when it commits a good deed.

6. The self can influence the mind negatively by controlling its thoughts and then one's actions: "We indeed created man; and We know what his soul whispers within him" (50:16).

وَلَقَدْ خَلَقْنَا الْإِنسَانَ وَنَعْلَمُ مَا تُوَسْوِسُ بِهِ نَفْسُهُ ۖ وَنَحْنُ أَقْرَبُ إِلَيْهِ مِنْ حَبْلِ الْوَرِيدِ - 50:16

The various states of the human self include:

- The self that encourages bad deeds
- The self that blames
- The assured self.

Aspect of the self that encourages bad deeds

This self encourages the individual to commit bad deeds. For example, see the verse, "Surely the soul of man incites to evil—except inasmuch as my Lord had mercy; truly my Lord is All-forgiving, All-compassionate" (Noble Qur'an, 12:53). This self can assume control over behaviours based on animal instincts, encouraging people to give in to their desires, except when religious guidance is stronger.

Aspect of the self that blames

There is also an aspect of the self that is vigilant about the risk of committing bad deeds. According to the Noble Qur'an, God declares: "No! I swear by the reproachful soul" (75:2). This aspect of the self is remorseful after a sin has been committed. It blames itself, causing discomfort, but it is also a sign of the strength of human conscience. The scholar Hasan al-Basri notes that believers often blame themselves by asking "Did I want this?", "Why did I do this?", or "Was this better than that?" (Qutb, 1996).

Aspect of the self that is reassured (the Assured Self)

This aspect of self is content with its Creator and at ease with its fate whether prosperity is given or withheld. The calm state of the Assured Self is due to a deep, unwavering faith in that which cannot be seen. Trust in God means that the self is not threatened by sadness or fear. The Noble Qur'an describes the Assured Self in this way: "O soul at peace, return unto thy Lord, well-pleased, well-pleasing! Enter thou among My servants! Enter thou My Paradise!" (89:27–30).

يَا أَيَّتُهَا النَّفْسُ الْمُطْمَئِنَّةُ - 89:27 ارْجِعِي إِلَىٰ رَبِّكِ رَاضِيَةً مَّرْضِيَّةً - 89:28 فَادْخُلِي فِي عِبَادِي - 89:29 وَادْخُلِي جَنَّتِي - 89:30

The concept of the Assured Self has many components. Please see below for different aspects that influence the development of the Assured Self.

Assured Self

- Acceptance of self: Accepting positive and negative aspects of oneself and having a positive self-concept.
- Feeling of subjective well-being: Taking advantage of the joys of life and satisfying basic needs and motivations. To have a sense of security and peace of mind, confidence, self-respect, and acceptance, loving others and having confidence in them, respecting and accepting others.
- Self-realisation: Having awareness of one's own strengths and capabilities and putting these into practice.

- Success in life: Undertaking professional work commensurate with one's individual capabilities, qualifications, and personal inclinations.
- Resilience: Meeting challenges and managing crises.
- Emotional balance: Being able to live with emotions, showing relevant feelings within the limits of appropriate self-control.
- Positivity: Having enthusiasm for life and facing it with optimism.
- Emotional assurance: Living while understanding and accepting that life is difficult. As the Noble Qur'an states: "Indeed, We created man in trouble" (90:4).

$$\text{لَقَدْ خَلَقْنَا الْإِنسَانَ فِي كَبَدٍ - 90:4}$$

- Integrity: Living in a way that avoids conflict between one's self and one's society.
- Loving one's own work: Having the ability to achieve and direct one's energies and behaviour towards wholesome and positive activities.
- Realism: Knowing and being aware of one's own abilities and determining the extent of ambition and potential.
- Ethics: Adopting values and principles that translate into one's own sense of integrity.
- Relationships: Building effective and lively relationships and interacting with others on the basis of respect and fairness.

We believe that Ershad coaching can support people to work towards their Assured Selves. It is a way of undertaking ongoing reflection and preparation as individuals strive to fulfil their missions. Below, we present the Alignment Wheel which is at the heart of the Ershad coaching framework.

The Alignment Wheel is embedded in the centre of the Ershad coaching framework. It can be employed at any phase of the conversational process. However, it is particularly well-suited for assessing pathways or options for appropriateness. We recommend using the Alignment Wheel with a learner once he or she has identified a number of pathways to pursue. Of course, the Alignment Wheel can be helpful to consider during the discovery phase (if a learner wishes to understand how to relate to the various relationships that are important to him or her). Again, the Alignment Wheel may be useful when a learner considers his or her future in the intention phase. And finally, behaviours and

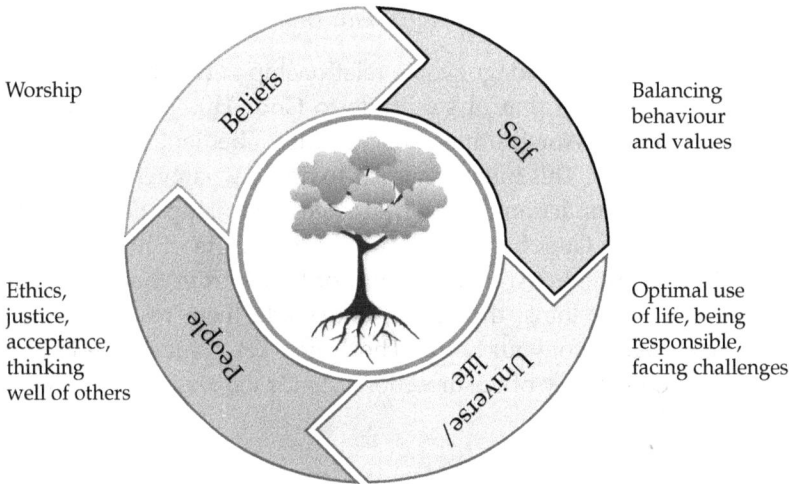

Worship

Balancing
behaviour
and values

Ethics,
justice,
acceptance,
thinking
well of others

Optimal use
of life, being
responsible,
facing challenges

Figure 8.2. Alignment Wheel.

mindset can be checked against the Alignment Wheel right at the end of the conversational process. We propose that it should be used where most appropriate in the opinion of learner and facilitator.

At appropriate moments during the Ershad coaching conversation, the learner should be given the opportunity to consider the Alignment Wheel. Through this process, the learner can evaluate his or her intent, behaviours, thoughts, and pathways. The first question can relate to the use of the Wheel itself:

- What does this model mean to you?
- How do you prioritise the four relationships?
- Where do you want to start?

There are four key relationships that can be addressed by using the Alignment Wheel:

- Beliefs
- Self
- Life
- People.

Relationship with beliefs

According to Islamic pedagogy, the relationship between a person and his or her Creator is that of servitude to God. This is demonstrated through worship. Worship means being fully obedient to God out of love towards Him. This intention leads to doing whatever pleases God in words, thoughts, actions, feeling, and deeds. Worship allows humans to draw closer to God, based on the common origin of human beings as has been testified: "And when thy Lord took from the Children of Adam, from their loins, their seed, and made them testify touching themselves, 'Am I not your Lord?' They said, 'Yes, we testify'—lest you should say on the Day of Resurrection, 'As for us, we were heedless of this'" (7:172).

وَإِذْ أَخَذَ رَبُّكَ مِن بَنِي آدَمَ مِن ظُهُورِهِمْ ذُرِّيَّتَهُمْ وَأَشْهَدَهُمْ عَلَىٰ أَنفُسِهِمْ أَلَسْتُ بِرَبِّكُمْ قَالُوا بَلَىٰ
شَهِدْنَا ۚ أَن تَقُولُوا يَوْمَ الْقِيَامَةِ إِنَّا كُنَّا عَنْ هَٰذَا غَافِلِينَ - 7:172

Worship is an innate need for every human being. It provides people with a higher sense of meaning. Acts of worship have a positive impact on the character, behaviour, and actions of a Muslim. Importantly, it also has an effect on the degree of alignment between the person and his or her community. Worship is a relationship in the form of servitude of people towards God. It is important because it can bring a sense of balance and harmony to the life of a Muslim, for the following reasons:

1. God is the Creator of all humankind and He knows what works for His creation and what harms them. Sending His message and guidance to humankind has been paving the path to success.
2. Faith in God is what settles into the heart and is translated through appropriate behaviours that are aligned with this faith and certainty. When the behaviour of a person is incompatible with his or her beliefs and values, he or she suffers anxiety, worries, and discomfort.
3. A Muslim would welcome an opportunity to reflect on his or her relationship with God. This is because a Muslim who wishes to achieve happiness and success in life will want to ensure a positive relationship with God.

If the learner chooses the relation with beliefs as an area to discuss, we can use the following questions in our coaching dialogue:

- "Tell me about your relationship with God."
- "How do you measure this relationship?"
- "How important is it to you to work out this relationship?"
- "What is the best image of your relationship with God?"
- "What are the actions you want to take in order to move forward and develop this relationship?"
- "What are the challenges that might get in the way of achieving your goals in this relationship?"

Relationship with self

God honours human beings. He created them with His divine hands and breathed His spirit into them. He commanded the angels to bow to human beings and He has preferred them over other creatures. God gave human beings blessed minds and common sense. God granted human beings trust after the universe declined to bear it: "We offered the trust to the heavens and the earth and the mountains, but they refused to carry it and were afraid of it; and man carried it" (33:72).

إِنَّا عَرَضْنَا الْأَمَانَةَ عَلَى السَّمَاوَاتِ وَالْأَرْضِ وَالْجِبَالِ فَأَبَيْنَ أَن يَحْمِلْنَهَا وَأَشْفَقْنَ مِنْهَا وَحَمَلَهَا الْإِنسَانُ
إِنَّهُ كَانَ ظَلُومًا جَهُولًا - 33:72

By the term "self", we are referring to the physical, psychological, and temperamental characteristics of a person. These include a person's opinions, beliefs, habits, talents, and social values. All of these inner characteristics impact on how a person interacts with others and the world.

The heathy self of a Muslim may include:

- Emotional maturity
- Preparedness to work continuously
- A sense of well-being, satisfaction, and pleasure
- A sense of security (an absence of fear)
- Self-confidence about the ability to cope with the demands of life
- Appreciation and respect for others and their rights and commitments
- Self-fulfilment and satisfaction with one's work

- Self-awareness and knowledge of one's own abilities
- Acceptance of shortcomings and recognition of individual differences
- Willingness to live in safety and harmony with others.

If the learner wishes to focus on his or her relationship with him- or herself, the facilitator can use the Alignment Wheel to ask the following questions:

- "How do you want to start talking about this aspect of your self?"
- "What are the personal values that govern your life?"
- "How do you present these values in your actions?"
- "Tell me about your relationship with your own self."
- "How do you measure this relationship?"
- "How important is it for you to work out this relationship?"
- "What is the best image of your relationship with yourself?"
- "How will you start to develop this relationship?"
- "What are the challenges that might stand in the way of achieving your goals in this relationship?"

Relationship with life

A person's relationship to life, from an Islamic perspective, revolves around the concept of "governance". In Arabic, the word that describes this relationship is *taskheer*, which means to do work and serve for free. Metaphorically, it means that God has enabled the use of the human universe to be beneficial to people in different areas of their lives without having to pay anything to the landlord, God, the sole owner of the universe.

This universe is here to serve human beings. However, God commands that it obeys human beings on the condition that they advocate for the rights of others. The law of *taskheer* increases and raises knowledge of the laws of the universe. This is why science is important for Muslims. When Muslims are well established in the knowledge of the true meaning and use of science and the philosophy of science, they will apply the laws of science as part of their faith in God.

If the learner is interested in exploring this question, it is beneficial to focus on how he or she interacts with life and the universe. How does the learner understand this relationship? And what is the learner doing to learn and develop an understanding of the world around him or her?

If the learner wishes to focus on the relationship with life, the facilitator can use the Alignment Wheel to ask the following questions:

- "How do you want to start talking about this aspect of yourself?"
- "What is your view of life?"
- "How do you see your relationship with the universe?"
- "Tell me about your relationship with the universe."
- "How do you measure this relationship?"
- "How important is it for you to work out this relationship?"
- "What is the best image of your relationship with the universe?"
- "How will you start to develop this relationship?"
- "What are the challenges that might stand in the way of your achieving your goals in this relationship?"

Relationship with other people

Relationship with others refers to treating other people in a kind manner that is characterised by tolerance and forgiveness. Islam requires a person to treat others kindly, gently, and without coercion. It prohibits ridiculing and showing contempt towards others. The Noble Qur'an commands that a person is obliged to greet others well, speak gently, and avoid harshness. It is a Muslim's duty to spread a sentiment of compassion, bonding, and altruism.

An essential aspect of a Muslim's role is cooperation. Cooperation is one of the most important features of social interaction because it includes joint work between members of a group. Cooperative people can live in harmony and peace based on mutual benefits. God has commanded that Muslims: "Help one another to piety and godfearing; do not help each other to sin and enmity" (5:2).

وَتَعَاوَنُوا عَلَى الْبِرِّ وَالتَّقْوَىٰ ۖ وَلَا تَعَاوَنُوا عَلَى الْإِثْمِ وَالْعُدْوَانِ ۚ وَاتَّقُوا اللَّهَ ۖ إِنَّ اللَّهَ شَدِيدُ الْعِقَابِ - 5:2

Cooperation among individuals reduces the degree of fear of failure and anxiety as well as the tendency to despair and lose hope. Instead, it provides a sense of tranquility and the safety of being part of the group.

Muslims are also expected to forgive others and have tolerance. They are commanded and encouraged to pardon especially when able to take revenge as this fosters social ties between the weak and the strong, allowing everyone to feel that they are part of a larger community. Good interpersonal relations are essential when building healthy communities that are free of conflict and social ills. Faith can play a role in helping people and offering them such good service, as the Prophet, peace be upon him, said: "No man is a true believer unless he desires for his brother that what he desires for himself" (Bukhari and Muslim, Book 1, Hadith 183).

If the learner is interested in exploring this relationship, it may be helpful to ask him or her to consider the relationships with important people in his or her life. Any personal relationships that are relevant to the topic of the coaching conversation can be discussed at this point.

If the learner wishes to focus on the relationship with others, the facilitator can use the Alignment Wheel to ask the following questions:

- "How do you want to start talking about your relationships with others?"
- "How important are your relationships?"
- "Who are the important people in your life?"
- "How would these decisions impact on your relationships?"
- "How do you measure your relationships with others?"
- "How will your [family member] be affected by your decisions?"
- "What impact will this have on your professional relationships?"
- "What are the challenges that might stand in the way of maintaining positive relationships with the important people in your life?"

Conclusion

In this chapter, we have focused on the most important aspect of the Ershad coaching framework. The Alignment Wheel provides the learner with a methodology for ensuring that his or her intention, pathways, and chosen efforts are aligned with his or her beliefs, values, relationships, and principles. In the next chapter, we will consider another essential ingredient of successful conversations using Ershad coaching: the "coaching way of being".

CHAPTER NINE

The coaching way of being

In the Ershad coaching framework presented in this book, we have proposed that effective coaching requires three elements: first, a set of skills; second, a conversational process; and finally, a coaching way of being. This chapter will consider the concept of the "coaching way of being" in detail. What we mean by this term is the essence of what a person *is*—as a human being. This is a rather abstract idea, but hopefully we will be able to share our understanding of this phrase with you in this chapter. Initially, we will present two views about particular ways in which coaches can interact with the people they work with. This will be followed by an exploration of how this can be understood in Islamic culture. The chapter will conclude with practical ideas about how to develop a "coaching way of being" in order to get the most out of the Ershad coaching framework.

Partnership principles

The partnership principles have been developed by Dr Jim Knight, a leading researcher in the field of coaching. According to Knight, there are a number of partnership principles that should characterise every coaching conversation (2007).

These seven principles are:

- Equality
- Choice
- Dialogue
- Praxis
- Voice
- Reciprocity
- Reflection.

Each of the principles is explained below:

Equality

Coaching should feel like a conversation between equals. Both facilitator and learner are of *equal value* as human beings, regardless of social or professional hierarchies.

Choice

The choices about the topic should be made by the learner. Facilitators should encourage the learner to make his or her own choices as far as possible. This principle includes the idea that the learner should choose to receive coaching. This means that we should avoid situations in which people are obliged to receive coaching against their will.

Dialogue

The coaching conversation should be experienced as a dialogue. This means that communication should flow both ways, and must not involve the facilitator telling the learner what to do. While the learner should be doing most of the talking, both parties should be contributing to the conversation.

Praxis

Coaching conversations should focus on actions and professional practice. In other words, the facilitator and learner must maintain a focus on the practical changes that the learner will make as a result of the conversation. This would mean that the facilitator should be regularly checking how the learner will be implementing new ideas.

Voice

The facilitator should interact with the learner in a way that encourages the learner to feel comfortable in saying what he or she is thinking and feeling. A skilled facilitator can create an environment in which learners are able to share their thoughts honestly and openly. The purpose of coaching is to allow learners to reflect on their fears as well as their hopes and dreams.

Reciprocity

A coaching conversation can bring benefits to both the facilitator and the learner. Both persons should feel that they are getting something positive from the conversation. Often facilitators report that they are learning too.

Reflection

Coaching is primarily an opportunity for quiet reflection, so the facilitator's role is to create a space and environment that is conducive to deep thinking, new ideas, and personal insights. Coaching should provide time for the learner to think.

Knight argues that implementing these seven principles can provide the basis of a strong, trusting, and mutually respectful relationship between the facilitator and the learner. The value of having such clearly identified principles is that it becomes possible for facilitators to evaluate their own practice. By ensuring that they are doing their best to follow the seven principles, facilitators increase their chances of constructing beneficial environments for productive conversations.

A coaching way of being

Ultimately, effective Ershad coaching may rely on the facilitator being able to adopt the partnership principles and start to embrace what we are calling a "coaching way of being" (van Nieuwerburgh, 2017). The phrase, "way of being" is borrowed from Carl Rogers (1980) who was a leading humanistic psychologist. He believed that every person could achieve his or her potential in life under the right conditions. Rogers's thoughts and experiments in the 1950s and 1960s very much inform our understanding. In the context of Ershad coaching, we will describe the "coaching way of being" as a particular set of beliefs and attributes that enhance the impact of coaching conversations. The coaching way of being is explained below. However, it is flexible and variable, so it should be understood as a broad concept, rather than specific guidelines.

The most effective facilitators are humble

Humility is at the heart of effective coaching, allowing the facilitator to build mutually respectful relationships with learners. This humility also underpins the facilitator's stance of "not knowing the answer" when it comes to the learner's topic. A humble person will find it easier to build strong, trusting relationships with their learners.

The most effective facilitators are confident in their ability to coach

Alongside a generally humble demeanour, a facilitator must nonetheless demonstrate confidence in the ability to support others through Ershad coaching. This self-confidence on the part of the facilitator will increase the hopefulness of the learner. We must remember that learners often seek support because they are uncertain of their ability to achieve their intentions. Working with a facilitator who is confident about the ability to support others to achieve more of their potential will definitely increase their positive expectations.

The most effective facilitators believe that their learners will achieve more of their potential

Powerful Ershad coaching conversations are often built on a shared and growing belief that the learner will be able to make the necessary changes in thinking and behaviour to achieve what is important to him or her. The facilitator's belief in the ability of the learner to do this can make all the difference. Part of the facilitator's belief that the learner will have the solutions and inspiration within him or her is demonstrated when the facilitator does not offer advice or suggestions.

The most effective facilitators treat others with respect

Part of the respectful approach is the ability to support others while believing that they have the intelligence and resources to identify the best way forward for themselves. It also includes being respectful of learners' opinions, culture, and preferences. This respect can be demonstrated by waiting silently for the learner to think.

The most effective facilitators have integrity

Ershad coaching may include discussions about business or organisational interests. Facilitators must place ethics and integrity at the heart of their professional practice. To put it simply, the facilitator should not make any decisions based on self-interest or personal profit when working with learners. In many ways, the facilitator should consider him- or herself as a role model when it comes to ethical behaviour.

The most effective facilitators care about people

One of the reasons many of us enjoy coaching is that we like people, and it is a great privilege to support others to lead meaningful and fulfilling lives. The best coaches are driven by the desire to support others, not by financial gain or organisational targets (This list is based upon ideas published in van Nieuwerburgh, 2017, pp. 173–175).

This is not a comprehensive list—and the "coaching way of being" may be shown in varied ways by different people. Not only that, each individual learner will experience the way of being differently. It is certainly difficult to define the term—and we believe that it varies across cultures and people. It is interesting to consider whether it is possible to "teach" this way of being to people. We are undecided about this. However, in our experience we have seen people who have intentionally developed their "coaching way of being" through reflective practice. So it seems to be the case that people can learn to enhance their way of being through practising coaching regularly if this is something of interest to them.

We believe that the partnership principles and the "coaching way of being" are important considerations that should inform the practice of Ershad coaching. Below, we will survey the necessary ethics and attributes of Ershad coaching facilitators.

Practical implications for Ershad coaching facilitators

1. Compassion and gentleness
   The facilitator should show good qualities, including the quality of mercy. Mercy means that the facilitator should be flexible, gentle, and lenient in his or her dealing with others. Leniency is one of the basic principles in the formation of human relationships in Islam. God says: "It was by some mercy of God that thou wast gentle to them; hadst thou been harsh and hard of heart, they would have scattered from about thee. So pardon them, and pray forgiveness for them, and take counsel with them in the affair; and when thou art resolved, put thy trust in God; surely God loves those who put their trust" (3:159).

   فَبِمَا رَحْمَةٍ مِّنَ اللَّهِ لِنتَ لَهُمْ ۖ وَلَوْ كُنتَ فَظًّا غَلِيظَ الْقَلْبِ لَانفَضُّوا مِنْ حَوْلِكَ ۖ فَاعْفُ عَنْهُمْ وَاسْتَغْفِرْ لَهُمْ وَشَاوِرْهُمْ فِي الْأَمْرِ ۖ فَإِذَا عَزَمْتَ فَتَوَكَّلْ عَلَى اللَّهِ ۚ إِنَّ اللَّهَ يُحِبُّ الْمُتَوَكِّلِينَ - 3:159

2. Patience
   Patience is needed in coaching and also for piety. The learner's goal is not likely to be achieved without patience. So this means that the facilitators need to be patient in their role, too. This attitude includes the recognition that in order to achieve high levels of expertise in coaching, it will be necessary to become a lifelong learner.

3. Humanity
   God sent the Prophet Muhammad (peace be upon him) as a guiding and promising harbinger for all people: "Say: 'O mankind, I am the Messenger of God to you all'" (7:158).

   قُلْ يَا أَيُّهَا النَّاسُ إِنِّي رَسُولُ اللَّهِ إِلَيْكُمْ - 7:158

So a facilitator should possess humanity and be willing to support all people, accepting everyone without discrimination.

We therefore recommend that facilitators of Ershad coaching will:

- Have a deep interest in human beings, their growth, and development. This means that facilitators will demonstrate genuine interest in the developmental needs and interests of their learners.
- Show empathy and compassion when communicating with learners. Facilitators can be inspired by the compassion and mercy shown in the Noble Qur'an.

- Have patience when working with their learners. This means allowing them time to reflect and come to their own conclusions.
- Be trustworthy in interactions with learners. Specifically, it will be necessary for facilitators to keep their conversations with their learners confidential. In addition, facilitators should do their best to keep any promises made to their learners.
- Have high expectations for their learners. This means that facilitators should encourage their learners to unlock more of their potential. At the same time, facilitators should also have high expectations of themselves.
- Promote humanity and equality. Facilitators should be open and accepting of everyone without discrimination.
- Think well of others (especially their learners), giving them the benefit of the doubt. This means assuming that their learners have positive intentions.
- Be humble in their interactions with their learners. The starting point for facilitators is to become aware of their own egos. The intention of Ershad coaching is simply to support others, not to enhance one's own reputation or standing.
- Respect the freedom and opinions of others. The role of the facilitator is to support and encourage the learner. Ershad coaching is not about controlling learners' thoughts or behaviours.
- Recognise that every person is responsible for him- or herself. It is not the role of the facilitator to save or rescue the learner.
- Believe that people are resourceful and able to identify their own pathways. This belief is demonstrated by facilitators when allowing learners to select their own pathways.
- Undertake the role to support others as part of their mission in life. The Ershad coaching framework should not be used purely on a commercial basis. Its function is to support people to guide themselves towards their correct paths.
- Act as role models in all their interactions with their learners. For Muslims, this includes living in ways that are based on teachings from the Noble Qur'an and the Sunnah while demonstrating faith and obedience to God.

By incorporating the three elements of effective coaching (skills, process, and a coaching way of being), the Ershad coaching framework can deliver these tangible benefits to learners:

- Improved health and satisfaction with life
- Enhanced ability to meet everyday challenges
- Support to overcome boredom or complacency
- Better use of existing skills and resources at work or at home
- Improved decision-making (personal and professional)
- Enhanced self-awareness, including recognition of one's strengths
- Better alignment between values and behaviours
- Strategies for living in a way that is compatible with principles and beliefs
- Understanding of the limits of personal responsibility in this life
- Increased self-confidence and belief in abilities
- Flexibility in dealing with others positively
- A growing sense of inner peace and calm.

We hope that readers of this book will be able to reflect on the extent to which they may already exhibit much of the coaching way of being outlined in this chapter. It is our belief that this way of being can be developed and enhanced by undertaking Ershad coaching. All that is required is a readiness to work on these aspects and a recognition that developing this way of being will involve practice, critical self-reflection, and an ongoing commitment to self-improvement.

Once people start to exhibit the coaching way of being, it will become clear that this is not just limited to coaching situations. It will transform how they see themselves and it will impact positively on interpersonal relationships. When people adopt this way of being, it can even start to impact on organisational cultures in a wide range of professional contexts (van Nieuwerburgh, 2016). So the way of being necessary for facilitators of Ershad coaching can enhance a person's ability to live a life of harmony and happiness, while helping others to do the same. We must remember that faith plays an important role in this by offering a vision of life that allows people to be grateful for their blessings, face challenges with patience, and look to the future with hope.

CHAPTER TEN

Conclusion

W e hope that you have found this book useful and that you can see positive ways in which this approach can impact on you and the people you interact with. This chapter will review the key aspects of the Ershad coaching framework and explain how we (the authors) have worked together to co-construct the approach. Finally, we will turn our gaze to the future, outlining our intention for Ershad coaching as it starts to be used within different contexts.

As we have seen, the Ershad coaching framework is designed to support individuals on journeys of discovery towards more aligned and purposeful selves. Ershad coaching is a methodology for facilitating the self-guidance of people who wish to work actively towards a positive intention for the future. As with other approaches, Ershad coaching can support the unlocking of potential and the pursuit of excellence. However, this approach focuses on alignment and is interested in helping individuals to identify and follow the path that is right for them.

A review of the Ershad coaching framework

As we have shown in this book, the Ershad coaching framework is made up of three components: the partnership conditions, the conversational process, and the Alignment Wheel.

Figure 10.1. Ershad coaching framework.

The partnership conditions

The partnership conditions are a prerequisite for effective coaching conversations. We have argued that a sense of mutual trust and respect is needed as the foundation of a strong relationship between the facilitator and the learner. This leads to a growing sense of collaboration in which each person considers the other to be a competent and trustworthy partner. In turn, this relationship creates the conditions for meaningful and reflective conversations.

The conversational process

A key component of the Ershad coaching framework is the conversational process. During this process, the facilitator demonstrates coaching skills and a way of being. The coaching skills include "listening with

purpose", "asking powerful questions", "summarising and paraphrasing", and "giving and receiving feedback". Effective facilitators will
demonstrate the "coaching way of being" during the conversational
process. In Ershad coaching, this coaching way of being is characterised
by patience, humanity, humility, and positivity. The facilitator should
adopt an open, non-judgmental approach in the spirit of partnership
and equality with the learner. This way of being supports the facilitator and learner to co-construct the reflective environment in which the
learner can safely explore true thoughts and feelings. The purpose of
this exploration is for the learner to identify the path that he or she
wishes to follow. There are four phases of the conversational process:

- **Discovery**: In this phase, learners are asked to reflect on themselves,
  their relationships, and their experiences. The facilitator supports the
  learners to better understand their existing resources. During this
  phase, it is helpful if learners can see their current situation from
  new or different perspectives.
- **Intention**: In this phase, learners are asked to turn their attention to
  the future. Facilitators support learners to articulate their intention
  for the future. In Ershad coaching, this is a very significant phase and
  the facilitator's role is to encourage learners to articulate their intention very clearly.
- **Pathways**: In this phase, learners are supported to explore a number
  of ways in which they might be able to move closer to their intention.
  The facilitator's role is to encourage the learners to generate as many
  ideas as possible. Following this, the learners should identify one
  pathway to pursue. The Alignment Wheel is usually introduced at
  this stage for the learners to assess whether the pathways are aligned
  with their beliefs and values.
- **Effort**: In the last phase of the conversational process, learners should
  consider what effort is required to follow their pathway. The facilitator's role is to help learners to relate the proposed effort to their
  intention. Learners will need to think about the necessary behaviours
  as well as ways of thinking.

The conversational process concludes at this point, allowing learners
an opportunity to start to put their thoughts into practice. When the
facilitator and learner meet again, they would start from the discovery
phase, focusing on what has happened since the previous session and
what learning has emerged. While the process has been presented as

linear and cyclical, in practice it is likely that the facilitator and the learner may move between the phases as appropriate for the situation. However, each conversation should cover all four phases, concluding with a decision about what actions will be undertaken between sessions.

At the very heart of the Ershad coaching framework is the Alignment Wheel. Its purpose is to support learners to make choices and decisions that are aligned with their own beliefs and values. When appropriate, the facilitator should ask learners questions relating to how their decisions will impact on important relationships in their lives. Learners can reflect on how a decision might affect the following:

- Relationship with their beliefs
- Relationship with self
- Relationship with life or the universe
- Relationship with important people in their lives.

The primary role of the Alignment Wheel is to ensure that the learner's self-selected pathway is the most appropriate one to follow. However, in practice, we have seen the Alignment Wheel used at various stages. For example, it can be helpful for some learners to reflect on these relationships at the discovery phase. This is particularly the case when learners are uncertain about what they would like in their future. An assessment of existing relationships with their beliefs, themselves, the universe, and other people can be a helpful starting point, leading to realisations about improvements that they might wish to make. At other times, the Alignment Wheel can be used to ensure that the learners' intention is consistent with their identity as Muslims and the important relationships in their lives. The visual representation of the tree that is at the centre of the Ershad coaching framework signifies growth and development along the "right path" as discussed in this book. Every learner will be able to identify his or her own "right path" through self-guidance.

At this point in the book, it may feel like the end of a particular journey. However, we hope that it is the start of a journey of self-discovery and your enhanced role in facilitating the development and growth of others. As authors, it is also a moment for us to reflect on our journey. Like you, our readers, it feels like the end of one journey and the beginning of another.

How the authors worked together

As we reflect back, we are reminded of our intention at the outset: to provide a culturally-relevant coaching framework for use in Islamic culture. This clear and shared intention was the powerful motivator that drove us to undertake and complete this sometimes challenging writing project. We also spent time, right at the outset, talking about how we would work together. Despite the fact that one of us lived in Kuwait and the other in England, we decided to meet in person as much as possible, but recognised that much of the work would need to be done virtually, over Skype and by email. We did much of the writing individually, and kept in touch regularly over Skype. We also organised a number of "writing weeks" in Dubai. We did some writing together during those weeks—but more importantly we explored our thinking, we challenged one another, and we made adaptations to the framework as a result. This text has been genuinely co-produced. Every concept and idea is something that has been discussed and agreed by both authors. Parts of the initial text were drafted in Arabic, other parts in English. We started without any particular model or framework in mind—we wanted to explore our shared and differing views. What we humbly present in this book emerged out of our experiences and our conversations.

We have learned so much during this period—about ourselves, about each other, and about the use of coaching in Islamic culture. We have both felt that the other has demonstrated many of the aspects of the coaching way of being that we have described. Humility was needed to acknowledge that we needed to learn so much during our collaboration. Curiosity spurred us on to find out more about this subject from existing scholarly works, from the Noble Qur'an, from the Hadith, and from practitioners in the field. We each brought a sense of appreciation and respect for the professional and personal experiences and insights of the other. As part of the writing process, we shared our thoughts and emerging frameworks with colleagues, clients, and friends. We had to take into account our own values, principles, and belief systems and share these with each other. When listening to these, we remained curious and non-judgmental so as to learn as much as possible from one another. Neither of us sought to impose our views or beliefs on the other.

To maintain a focus on practice, we invited case studies of a range of coaching interventions delivered in Islamic contexts. These are presented in the final chapter of this book (Chapter Eleven). We studied these carefully and made refinements to our framework as a result. Each of us tested the Ershad coaching framework with clients and colleagues. The entire writing process has been characterised by a constant exchange of ideas and sharing of experiences. It has felt like we were undertaking an important mission.

Looking forward

As we look forward, we are optimistic. We hope that the Ershad coaching framework will play a part in supporting growth, development, and learning in Islamic culture. However, we believe that this framework may have universal application. It should be effective in any situation in which alignment is needed. This framework supports individuals to make decisions about their own growth and development while taking into account the impact of these decisions on their relationships and environment.

Furthermore, we believe that becoming a facilitator of Ershad coaching will have its own benefits. There is some argument for the facilitator to develop him- or herself as a role model. Underpinning the message of the Noble Qur'an is that human beings should better themselves and their societies. Being a facilitator of Ershad coaching is one way of supporting this intention. We recommend that the facilitator reflects on his or her own mission or purpose, and then invests effort towards this. Sharing this with a learner may be helpful at the start of the conversational process. What is your intention in relation to the learner? What is your intention of being a facilitator of Ershad coaching?

We want to conclude by recalling the importance of the relationship in all coaching interactions. We include both the professional and human aspects of relationship in this reminder. In Ershad coaching, the relationship must take precedence over any key performance indicator, target, or objective. This type of conversation is ultimately a very human interaction between two people.

Looking towards the future, our hope is that this Ershad coaching framework will help to build greater understanding between cultures. We also hope that Ershad coaching will remind people of their missions and purpose. The process will also encourage people to take responsibility. It is likely that Ershad coaching will improve well-being and performance. Coaching has been shown to have positive impacts on individuals and organisations (Grant, Passmore, Cavanagh, & Parker, 2010; Passmore & Fillery-Travis, 2011; Theeboom, 2016; Theeboom, Beersma, & van Vianen, 2014), and on education (van Nieuwerburgh, 2012; van Nieuwerburgh & Barr, 2016). Our hope is that the Ershad coaching process will deliver positive outcomes on personal, organisational, and societal levels.

CHAPTER ELEVEN

Case studies and personal stories

In this chapter, we will survey a number of case studies that demonstrate how coaching is already being used with care and sensitivity in various contexts. Each case study highlights a particular aspect of the complexities, challenges, or rewards of using coaching in Islamic culture. They all follow the same format: brief contextual information, an exploration of the case study, and some learning points that emerged. Every case study presents some implications for coaching practice in Islamic culture. We conclude this chapter with two personal stories that demonstrate the potential transformative effect of coaching.

Coaching in professional contexts

We will start by considering the use of coaching within professional contexts. This is an area of growth internationally and is the focus of current interest and research (van Nieuwerburgh, 2016). In the first case study, an internal executive coach at a university in the Gulf region explores the challenge of coaching a member of staff who is more familiar with didactic or directive forms of professional support.

Case study: Coaching a high-potential Gulf national in a university context

Author: Performance and learning partner at a university

Short contextual information

A high-potential professional and Gulf national volunteered to take part in a pilot coaching programme delivered by internal coaches with the aim of supporting career development of local staff within the university. The coaching programme was seen as an alternative solution to the widely preferred, traditional way of developing skills which was mainly through classroom training.

What happened?

During the introductory session my main objective was to build rapport and set responsibilities and expectations of the coaching sessions. I started by explaining the framework of the coaching programme as a means of supporting career development. Through this initial conversation, the topics that emerged were apprehension about leadership roles and some concerns about work-life balance. The main challenge was to support the coachee to define the desired outcome. This required patience and an insistence on my part. In my role as coach, I asked questions over and over so that the desired outcome became clear to both of us. At some point, I realised that the concern about leadership roles was a philosophical concern with no immediate need for action. We therefore revisited the session's initial goal. At that moment I felt the need to be open and check if the coachee had a burning topic to explore. It was my feeling that otherwise the coaching sessions would not be effective. This led us to the second topic about work-life balance. Now aware of the challenge of defining a desired outcome, I decided to adopt a solution-focused approach by asking a future-focused question which proved to be quite effective. Along the way there was an expectation from the coachee to be given advice. She was keen to be offered solutions. I often received the following response as a result of my coaching questions: "If I knew the solution, I would have solved the problem." Being able to enrich my coaching practice with additional coaching techniques, I had the opportunity to keep the conversation flowing when it seemed rather stuck and pass the "ownership" of exploring solutions and new ways of thinking or acting to the coachee. More specifically, at a point when the conversation seemed to lead nowhere and no additional insights were generated, I introduced a practical activity where the coachee had to stand in one position and take on the role of observer. This generated new insights and additional options. The way forward then seemed easier and more straightforward as the coachee had actually experienced the options in a more experiential way.

Another important parameter of the coaching relationship was to build rapport and create a trusting and safe environment and this needed some extra time in the initial sessions. However, once achieved, the challenge was to control it in the most delicate way so that it would not take too much time out of the core coaching conversation. More specifically, since the particular coachee had not experienced coaching before, I noticed some difficulty in opening up and starting the conversation. During the initial session, my questions created an atmosphere of embarrassment and many "don't knows". I could sense that questioning was not only an unfamiliar process but also a way of breaking some "walls" of privacy. Frequent reassurances while also offering support mainly through the tone of my voice, warm nodding, and empathetic eye contact eventually created a trusting atmosphere. I recall that after the initial session that overran by half an hour, the coachee admitted that she had never had the chance to talk to a "stranger" like that before--not even to close friends. This was the first important step of relationship-building. However, during the later sessions this initial stage became a challenge as the coachee was feeling more comfortable and therefore enjoyed talking more since I had passed the "privacy test". Keeping this momentum but refocusing on the main objective of the coaching relationship had to be well balanced.

Learning and observations

A clear explanation of what coaching is and how it differs from mentoring is essential to begin with. This clarifies and sets expectations on behalf of both parties. Building a trusting relationship is very important for this culture, being mainly "high context" but at the same time quite private.

Practical implications

- Coaches should clearly explain the difference between coaching and mentoring and set relevant expectations.
- Coaches should invest time to build the relationship in the first sessions but make sure you manage the rapport throughout the coaching assignment.
- Coaches should remain flexible in using different coaching techniques and experiment with more experiential ones to support the generation of new insights.
- Coaches should be patient and resist offering advice or solutions.

In another case study that echoes some of the issues raised above, an experienced executive coach encounters challenges while rolling out a coaching programme for aspiring leaders in the UAE.

Case study: Coaching UAE nationals in leadership positions
Author: Charmaine Klima, senior leadership development advisor in a UAE oil and gas company

Short contextual information

A semi-structured approach to coaching was developed for coaching talent pool individuals within a large oil and gas organisation. The organisation is undergoing intensive efforts to develop UAE nationals in leadership positions. The organisation had recently established a talent development centre (TDC) for assessment of talent against established leadership competencies. A number of talent pool members were nominated to participate in coaching sessions at the completion of their TDC feedback session in an effort to lay the foundations for developing a coaching culture within the organisation, to develop action plans, and identify the future career aspirations of these talent pool members.

What happened?

As the lead coach and in order to ensure a uniform approach by the coaching team, I developed a framework for semi-structured post-TDC coaching conversations, the purpose of which was to provide an opportunity to:

- Review the TDC development feedback received by the nominee
- Examine the response to feedback and provide context for its application outside the assessment centre
- Identify individual career aspirations
- Identify specific future development opportunities, goals, and action plans to support their aspirations.

The nature of these sessions was discussed at the opening of each coaching conversation, along with the expectation that the content of the session would be confidential. However, the aspirations of the individuals, where appropriate and with their specific permission, could be used to inform the organisation's succession planning process to ensure consideration was given to both the organisation's and individuals' goals for career development.

During many of these sessions, the most significant challenge encountered for both parties was in defining career aspirations along with the accompanying development opportunities, goals, and action plans to support these aspirations. Often, it was the first time individuals had given any deliberate consideration to their future goals. For many, the response was simply, "Whatever the company wants", or "Whatever is decided for me". When delving deeper into what these individuals would want for themselves if given the choice, it also became apparent that many were feeling the pressure to fit into family expectations of what their future careers, mainly defined by title, should be.

A common response was, "It is in our culture to want to be told what to do and what we need to do [so if you] tell me exactly what you want then I will do it as this is what we expect in our culture." Deeper discussion, the use of examples and storytelling, challenging and questioning was required by coaches over an extended period of sessions to encourage the formation and clarification of individuals' aspirations. Furthermore, although the company has adopted a philosophy of empowering female nationals to pursue leadership opportunities, it was not uncommon to encounter women who felt their voice and influence were not being heard or they were being overlooked for advancement opportunities. While they also felt the pressure of family expectations as to what their future careers should be, often they felt additional pressures and even limitations, because they felt there was a general anticipation that their family commitments may interfere with their work. Faced with such situations, some of these women also felt challenged in creating a clear picture of what they would want in their future. Other women were very clear about what their aspirations were. However, they were equally unclear if these were realistic and achievable given the environmental pressures. In these situations, coaches were encouraged to explore topics such as self-esteem, self-image, and assertiveness and to encourage individuals to look for examples of success, such as role models.

For those who were able to define their aspirations, when asked whether they had or would discuss this with their manager, the answer was often "No". Similarly, when discussing action plans, individuals who stated a desire to be nominated for more specific leadership development opportunities were hesitant to discuss this with their managers. This was based on the assumption that the company would decide what opportunities would be given to whom. It is not the norm to ask as there is a cultural expectation that the company will take care of employees' careers for them. As a result, individuals don't see the need to define their future career goals and action plans. However, often these same individuals were experiencing feelings of frustration at not being given the opportunities they wanted or required in order to progress their careers.

Learning and observations

A uniform approach to coaching conversations was useful as the team was able to provide valuable data, such as career aspirations, back into the succession planning process. Although the term "coaching" is used often in organisations, individuals may need time to understand the true nature of coaching. For some, influencing one's own career outside the pressure of family expectations, organisational paradigms, and cultural norms may be unfamiliar. It proved useful in this instance for coaches to be patient and develop the individuals' aspirations over a number of sessions. For those able to define their aspirations, it is common to remain silent on what they feel would be required to reach their goals and to express a desire to be given development opportunities. This can be a cause of frustration and it is important to gain commitment to action to move through this frustration.

Practical implications

- Coaches should spend time discussing and agreeing the role and responsibilities of each party in a coaching conversation.
- Coaches must practise patience and allow ideas and themes to develop at the pace required by each individual.

- Increased frequency of sessions at the outset may be required for those struggling to form their own picture of their goals and aspirations.
- Good rapport is essential from the outset to ensure the coach can delve deeper into areas which the individual may not have deliberately considered before.

Brief biographical information

Charmaine Klima | MBA | MCIPD | CAHRI | BPS (A&P)
With an international career spanning defence, private and government sectors, oil and gas, security, global sporting events, and entrepreneurship, Charmaine has held positions of immense responsibility and leadership since an early age. A founding member of the "Women's Excellence Group" Mentoring Committee, Charmaine is a chartered member of the Chartered Institute of Personnel Development (MCIPD), a certified professional member of the Australian Human Resources Institute (CAHRI), a registered psychological test user and administrator (BPS A&P), and certified in the application of various psychometric instruments. Her areas of interest include: leadership development coaching, leading in the multi-generational workplace; building high performing teams, and organisational culture and diversity.

In the following case study, an expatriate coach working in the Gulf region undertakes a successful coaching conversation and learns about the concept of *ihsan* through her coachee.

Case study: Coaching with *ihsan*
Author: Helen Ashley, independent coach, facilitator, and consultant

Short contextual information

This case study took place within a newly established and rapidly growing education and research-focused organisation based in the Gulf region. The workforce is made up of a broadly equal split of Gulf nationals and expatriates, mainly coming from North America, Europe, and Asia. At the time this case study took place, a small-scale coaching pilot was taking place within the organisation with the aim of supporting employees with performance improvement and career development.

In general, coaching clients were referred to the coach by their line manager in order to focus on a specific performance or development-related issue. Issues might have been identified by coaching clients themselves or by a member of line management, a client, or a colleague. In this case study, the coachee is Maha, a female Gulf national. She is a graduate in her twenties working in a client-facing technical project management function. I was the coach--a British female professional development specialist in her forties based in the organisation's human resources function. Coaching conversations took place in English, the business language of the organisation.

What happened?

Prior to the first coaching session, Helen met Maha's manager, Faisal, to discuss his reasons for making the coaching referral and to find out more about the outcomes he was hoping for. Faisal said that he had recommended Maha as a candidate for coaching to improve her interpersonal skills and the way she dealt with clients. Faisal said that Maha was very good at the technical side of her role, but that clients complained about her relatively abrupt manner and poor listening skills. Faisal said he was concerned that Maha felt under pressure and could not manage her stress levels well, and that she did not seem to recognise this about herself. She was not able to reflect on the role she played in building good relationships with her colleagues. In short, she was technically very competent, but would not be able to progress to more senior roles within the team unless she could learn to get on better with clients and collaborate more.

Maha agreed to a first meeting. She was curious about coaching but worried that she had been singled out. Most of the first session was spent discussing the coaching process, and in particular going over what records would be kept and who those records would be shared with. Maha wanted a lot of reassurance about the confidentiality of the coaching conversations, and the

role her line manager played in the process. Due to some bad experiences resulting from being too open in her conversations with colleagues, she had learned to be more guarded in what she said. We agreed to plan for five ninety-minute meetings at regular intervals over the next three months, at times and in locations that best suited Maha. She would send me calendar invitations at least one week in advance.

Maha chose to meet in my office in the morning, before starting her working day. The exact start time of the session remained flexible between around 7:00 and 8:00am. Over the five sessions, we unpacked Maha's role, the things she enjoyed doing, and some of the aspects she found more challenging. We also spent an almost equal amount of time speaking about Maha's family, her relationships with her sisters and her parents, her faith, and her life within the community. It did not make sense to Maha to discuss her work-life in isolation, outside the wider context of her life. Where I saw a number of different discrete strands in Maha's life—the compartments I know as work, family, social, and so on—she did not. She saw no inherent conflict between personal and professional. If her mother was ill, she might decide it was important to stay home to look after her; if there was an important work deadline, she might decide it was important to stay late at the office—each situation would be considered within the context of the whole. Any work-based rules, for example, "office hours", were open to flexible interpretation within this wider context.

At first, Maha was quite clear that her character and personality were fixed and could not be changed. Her role in the organisation meant that she must be shown respect by her colleagues. People who did not show appropriate respect should be corrected by their managers. As we dug deeper into this issue, she began to consider that there might be more than one approach to any situation, and that she might have a part to play in influencing the ways colleagues and clients behaved towards her.

Maha's breakthrough moment came when she introduced the concept of "ihsan" into our conversations. She explained that *ihsan* is "doing beautiful things", by taking one's inner faith and showing it in action. She said that my coaching showed *ihsan* in the way I always spoke and behaved respectfully, and that she had started to plan ways of bringing *ihsan* into her interactions with clients and colleagues. As she spoke about her ideas with increasing clarity and resolve, I started to relate what she said to familiar concepts like empathy, active listening, and reflection. It occurred to me that the principles of *ihsan* and the idea of being able to coach with *ihsan* were important lessons for me to learn.

Learning and observations

The principles and aims of coaching are not universally understood. I needed to take time to explain what coaching is, how it works in practice, and to be detailed about the expectations and commitments required of both coach and coachee. I had to remain mindful that many of my ideas and behaviours are culturally specific, and that people from different cultures can see things very differently. The coaching sessions took place in my native language, English. Maha's English is excellent, but it is not her mother tongue. I had to check and check again to be confident that I understood her meaning as deeply as possible during our coaching conversations.

Practical implications

- Faith is personal and individual. Be mindful of making assumptions about what someone might think or how they might behave.
- Some people find it difficult to express their discomfort with a coach of the opposite sex. Be sensitive to this and facilitate the most positive coaching experience possible.
- Time is a cognitive construct and different cultures measure punctuality in different ways. Be open to these differences and challenge your own ways of thinking.

Brief biographical information

Helen Ashley has over twenty-five years' experience in developing people and organisations as a coach, trainer, facilitator, and consultant. She has worked for prestigious organisations in both the public and private sectors based in the UK, Europe, North America, and the Middle East. Her research activities focus on developing more effective communication strategies that can enrich and stimulate collaboration and team working. She has delivered presentations and workshops on this topic at national and international conferences, and is currently coaching at an NHS acute foundation trust. For more information she can be contacted at helen.ashley@yahoo.co.uk.

In the final case study of this section, a leadership consultant shares the findings of his research and experiences of executive coaching in Saudi Arabia.

Case study: The experience of Western coaches working with Saudi Arabian clients

Author: Ronnie Zachary Nganwa, leadership development professional working in the Middle East

Context

In a drive to meet a vision for 2030, where Saudi Arabia becomes the heart of the Arab and Islamic world through increased investment and diversification, several organisations are focused on developing leaders from within the local population.

My coaching practice came to Saudi Arabia to support this. Soon I recognised how diminished my Western cultivated certainty was and how challenges seemed to multiply. Consider for instance, the difference in emphasis religion has in Saudi Arabia, at a cultural level, compared to that found within Western society, and how to deal with that when coaching within organisations or government agencies.

This led me to undertake a study of cross-cultural coaching focused on what Western coaches perceived to be important when working with Saudi coachees.

The experiences shared in this case study may be helpful to coaches as they consider and refine their Western-rooted approaches. The context-specific guidance, competencies, and aptitudes presented allow for the development of a framework of practice to emerge for those embarking on assignments in the Gulf region.

Findings

1. Approach to coaching

   Deep listening used to reveal the coachees' reality and what they're experiencing is critical to successful practice. This is particularly crucial when the coaching emphasises ownership of action, as is often the case with organisation-based performance coaching. Formidable concepts such as "Wasta" (loosely defined as favouring those from within one's family, tribe, or network, particularly when it comes to upward social mobility) often emerge. The work for the coach is in combating this limiter, without allowing it to be an excuse for inaction.

2. Saving face and conflict avoidance
Coaches must also consider the need to save face that emerges with clients, often coupled with conflict avoidance. It becomes difficult to challenge within interventions, particularly where the participant is unwilling to engage with it. This calls for strong rapport remaining in place if any work is to progress. Several coaches, particularly those working within organisations, have sensed their challenges being tolerated, with one coach describing, "I think the Saudis tend to say, oh here we go, another Westerner coming in and telling me their ideologies, let me just ride the storm and wait until they go and then I can just do what I want to do anyway."

3. The importance of religion
Religion often emerges within coaching conversations where I have found it to be used, in the main, as a guide for decision-making or commitment to action. Coachees will revert to it as the determiner of how they should behave and crucially the level of control they have in their lives, with regards to change. You can expect to hear, "This is how the Qur'an tells us to be." A distinction does need to be made between religion and culture. One of the coaches describes using knowledge of the Noble Qur'an and the Hadiths which describe behaviours, specifically how people deal with each other.

With this, he recognised his knowledge as leverage in gaining movement with coachees by focusing appropriate challenges to "not so useful cultural constraints" and being careful when approaching religious constraints, seeing these as being far more intertwined with the coachee's personal values.

4. Cross-gender interaction
The male coach may expect some restriction on physical contact with women. If there is a requirement for contact, it is suggested that there may be a need to discuss the cultural barrier during contracting to ensure it is not inadvertently breached. Aside from promoting comfort for both, it demonstrates cultural awareness and promotes credibility. This has become a point of great conversation within the coaching communities in the region, considering the ambitions to increase the number of women within the workplace and in leadership positions.

5. Family

I find that discussion of family, particularly the ambitions held from the family, come much quicker with Saudi clients than with clients from other cultures.

Family remains fundamental to how the culture operates so coaches have to respect and hold that in warm regard. One coach offered, "Family is front and centre here backed up by faith." Many coaches find that reference to their own family offers some advantage as the coaching alliance begins to form.

Conclusion

These discoveries lead to an appreciation of the complexity in cross-cultural coaching and raise awareness of the development needed to hold coaching well in this context.

With Western coaching becoming aware of such critical, cross-cultural nuances, more effective coaching relationships may materialise and lead to individual and aggregate improvements in Saudi society.

Practical implications

1. **Leverage cultural values**: By recognising the influence of culture on personal values, reference to action to move towards a goal or change is better received if positioned with the appropriate cultural values of the region.
2. **Systemic approach facilitates new thinking**: Remaining mindful of factors external to the immediate situation described by a coachee, the coach becomes instrumental in highlighting the possible impact of culture upon a coachee's issues and facilitates new thinking.
3. **Mindful of coachee expectations**: Often the coachee is looking for direction and advice, whereas the coach works to encourage coachee generated ideas. In positioning the interaction, it is helpful to remain mindful of cultural expectations of the "helper" being a wiser, more experienced advisor.

Brief biographical information

Ronnie Zachary is a change consultant and executive coach, operating within the technology, finance, and energy sectors across EMEA.

He holds a master's degree in coaching and behavioural change which supports his work developing Middle Eastern leaders as they reshape their operations. His areas of interest include: leadership and cross-cultural coaching, team development, and organisational design.

Coaching in educational contexts

Coaching has a significant contribution to make within educational settings (van Nieuwerburgh, 2012; van Nieuwerburgh & Barr, 2016). In the first case study in this section, two educators consider respectful ways of working in Islamic culture. Using the idea of a "third culture", the authors present a model for introducing coaching across a school setting.

Case study: Coaching in third culture spaces

Authors: Jan Alen, senior consultant, Growth Coaching International, Australia, and Annette Wilson, executive principal, Australian International School, United Arab Emirates

Short contextual information

The Australian International School is located in Sharjah in the United Arab Emirates. It was the first Australian school to be established in the Middle East and was formed through a partnership between the Al Sharif Investment Trading Group and the government of Queensland, Australia. The purpose was to provide a quality school that would respect the culture, religion, and language of the people of the UAE. It is the intention of the owners that the school ensures the highest quality in teaching and learning across the Australian curriculum while offering equally high-quality programmes in the teaching of Arabic and Islamic studies.

What happened?

We have worked over time to create what we call a "culture of the third way". This is not just an Australian school sitting on the sands of Sharjah, nor is it a private Arab school that happens to use an Australian curriculum. For the school to be effective, we continuously work to develop this cultural space which values all people who work here. This requires a focus on communication, development of a common purpose, and the building of trust and relational capital.

We have implemented four waves of training for coaches at the Australian International School. We began training members of the executive team in 2013 and expanded this to all heads of department in 2014 and then to teacher leaders in early 2014. This has enabled all leaders to work with a common and consistent coaching framework and language in development and performance conversations with team members and direct reports. The most recent round has seen A.I.S. train all eighty-four teachers in a peer coaching programme. A number of senior leaders are also recipients of one-to-one individual coaching. Jan Alen, GCI senior consultant, facilitated the series of coaching programmes in partnership with the executive principal and the leadership team.

Learning and observations

It is interesting to reflect that, whilst our view of important concepts such as leadership seem to be culturally based, the concept of coaching seems to fit very comfortably across cultures. The value of a coach working with a colleague to enhance teaching performance was strongly supported across the school. A case in point is where a teacher of Arabic chose an Australian teacher as his learning partner in the peer coaching programme specifically to learn more about contemporary pedagogical practices which he noted were very different to his training as a teacher or his own school experience.

Practical implications

- It is important to be respectful of issues that may be important within the UAE culture (e.g., we would suggest only single sex coaching partners).
- We chose to do this training at the weekend so we could invite the maximum number of teachers. It was important then to do this for our Muslim colleagues on the Saturday. Friday is prayer day in the UAE.
- This highlights another important consideration which is to maximise choice, ownership, and engagement. For example, teachers chose their peer coaching partner and the area of practice they wanted to focus on.

Brief biographical information

Jan Alen is senior consultant with Growth Coaching International and director of Jan Alen Consulting and has worked in the area of educational leadership for over twenty-five years, including the successful development and implementation of system-wide leadership capability standards and frameworks, designing and delivering mentoring and work shadowing programmes, aspirant programmes, and programmes supporting principal well-being. Jan was the foundational director of programmes at the Queensland Education Leadership Institute and director at the Institute of Educational Administration in Victoria.

Annette Wilson is the executive principal of the Australian International School, Sharjah, a K-12 school with an enrolment of 1362 students. Annette has extensive experience in providing professional development for educational leaders and was the designer of the assessment centre used to identify high performing candidates as part of a selection system for principals of large schools. Annette has also worked on research projects to identify those competencies that most differentiate between average and high performing principals. Annette was a member of the Centre for Leadership Excellence in the Queensland Department of Education, Training and Employment.

In the following case study, we will consider how coaching is used to support executive education students undertaking leadership and management courses in the Gulf region.

Case study: Coaching to support an executive education student

Author: Esther Chater (FInstLM)

Short contextual information

All students undertaking a leadership and management course delivered at a university in the Gulf region are given access to executive coaching. The coach contracts directly with the coachee to work together in a confidential setting over a six-month period to address the coachee's specific needs.

What happened?

I was allocated Mohamed and given a copy of his CV for background information. Getting to know him was the most critical aspect for me as I was aware it would also include a steep learning curve in terms of cultural understanding and appreciation on my part. Although I had been working in the Middle East for a number of months, I still came across different perspectives and ideologies. I felt a sense of responsibility to him, to get the most out of our sessions for his own personal and professional benefit. I view coaching as a two-way process in raising awareness, noticing and describing what is happening, and sharing my own experiences.

Learning and observations

I remember the first meeting with Mohamed. He was eager and keen to understand what coaching was and what he could get out of it. After building rapport and contracting it appeared clear what he wanted to work on. This changed as we progressed. He appeared confident, but reserved. He was technically competent and well educated, had several years' working experience in his industry, but felt that he was being constantly overlooked for promotion. While discussing this further, it emerged that he had not enquired to find out why he had been overlooked for promotion. He responded that he felt it not appropriate, as it was not something he would do. He was also concerned that he would not know what to say to the chief executive who routinely had working lunches within the organisation. I noted comments in my own reflective journal that he appeared emotionally sensitive and affected by self-doubt. The critical moment I could sense was when I asked how he could improve if he wasn't aware of the reasons for being overlooked. He responded his manager was responsible for putting forward candidates for promotion. As a result of the conversation, he decided to ask for a mentor to support him with his career development.

To continue to build rapport and ongoing commitment, I followed up after each session with an email summary of our discussion and outcomes that we had agreed. This often included some supportive reading and or video clips. I wanted to use a variety of learning styles by taking this approach to add greater understanding. Formative and summative feedback from the coachee at the end of each session was good: *"Kind and continuous follow up. I really enjoyed talking to you and your listening. The thing that impressed me most was your dedication and commitment for* the sessions and endeavor to help me overcome my gaps";"I am hoping that our professional relationship that we have is kept forever. I won't forget all the effort you have put in to push me to this level."

Meeting face-to-face or Skype/telephone was used for subsequent coaching sessions. Face-to-face meeting at venues was always an option for the coachee to decide where. This was inevitably in a mall in the UAE, on a Thursday afternoon. As long as the meeting place was confidential and where it put the coachee at ease—that worked for me. He brought his wife to be introduced to me on the final session. This made me feel honoured in one respect. At the end of this final face-to-face session, everything had gone well, and the coachee was more confident and at ease with how things were progressing at work. As we suggested to keep in touch, even if via LinkedIn, I automatically went to shake hands. He did shake (somewhat reluctantly), and said, "That is not part of our culture."

I have learned much from working with this client in terms of my own practice and am pleased I have witnessed real development for Mohamed, which has been wonderful to observe.

Practical implications

- Time should be taken to build the relationship.
- Be cautious when using confronting techniques.
- Be aware that the role of destiny will be very significant.

Brief biographical information

Esther Chater, FInstLM, has over twenty years' experience developing people and facilitating change within both public and private sector organisations. She has worked in the UK and Middle East, in the education, health, banking, and airline sectors. She has an MBA and a further master's-level qualification in executive coaching and mentoring. Esther enjoys helping clients to access their own self-awareness to facilitate their own learning. She works as a consultant and is a fellow of the Institute of Leadership and Management.

One-to-one coaching

In the following case study, we consider the use of coaching with the specific purpose of developing resilience. The author of the case study presents a particular psychological intervention that has been designed for Islamic culture.

Case study: A coaching conversation with a London-based Muslim professional

Author: Dr Aneta D. Tunariu, School of Psychology, University of East London

Short contextual information

Inbar is a Muslim woman in her thirties with an established PR and events planning business in central London seeking coaching input to review and strategically expand the reach and remit of her business. The coaching work with Inbar was used, alongside other cases and resources, to inform the development and piloting of a new well-being and resilience programme within an Islamic context (Tunariu, 2017). The iNEAR coaching for resilience framework is informed by principles and research from existential positive psychology, developmental coaching, and psychotherapy. Its aim is broadly concerned with the acquisition of skills for growth and flourishing and it is structured around new knowledge about the individual; emotional resources and emotional intelligence; awareness of values, options, and choice; responding with growth "in spite of ..." (Tunariu, 2015).

iNEAR sits in alignment with the Ershad coaching framework proposed by van Nieuwerburgh and Allaho in the present book. The two consider similar core principles such as *intention* (awareness; deliberate self-positioning; trusting the intention), *effort*, and *possibilities*, each conceived as opportunities which coaching can open up to a holistically understood *self-system*. The chief distinctiveness of iNEAR as an integrative positive psychology and coaching framework within an Islamic context is threefold: (i) it is specifically designed to address emotional well-being and the capacity for resilience; (ii) it is enveloped by the view of the Islamic dialogue as inherently existential; (iii) it can be used as part of a wider group intervention (Tunariu & El Guenuni, 2016) or to scaffold individual coaching sessions. This case study considers its use in a one-to-one coaching conversation.

What happened?

Early interventions in the coaching process with Inbar focused on taking stock of what is being done, what works well, and on co-authoring a set of goals and objectives as part of the stretch management strategy. Inbar selected me as a coach with a background in existential coaching psychology, without a distinct reason apart from a sense that she wanted a holistic approach to her leadership and management review. As we explored her understanding of this it emerged that for Inbar the question "Where next as a company?" was intertwined with "Where next as a leader?" and "Where next as Inbar?" The latter came as a curious and pleasant surprise for the coachee. Moreover, what also became clear as the sessions progressed was the pivotal role the Islamic philosophy and way of life actually held for Inbar. This realisation shifted and widened the focus of our discussions and indeed the nature of the coaching interventions to follow. These included attention to challenges Inbar felt she was encountering in her attempts to observe Islamic teaching and aspects of her professional lifestyle. Our explorations for responses to these dilemmas primarily hinged on seeing Islamic alternatives as context-related improvements or additions to, rather than an automatic dismissing-critique of Western approach to business or to coaching matters. For instance, balancing moral decisions within a business setting and the self-narrative about a "good" and moral way of conducting one's life; or balancing economic objectives and the risk of sliding into materialist concerns and their circularity and narrowness of vision.

Learning and observations

Organically, the core structure of the iNEAR framework emerged as a useful scaffolding to bridge the intersection between the inner congruence of Islamic values and actions based on this developing knowledge. The "i" in the iNEAR sets the platform for the recognition of self in relation to the spiritual, the philosophical, and to our deliberate actions towards discipline, acceptance, harmony, and growth. "N" celebrates new knowledge about oneself, its contribution to one's inner psychological world, and the importance of trusting one's (personal and professional) intention. "E" refers to expanding one's emotional intelligence and one's ongoing repertoires of emotional resourcing; here, for instance, Inbar identified the time of prayer, a habit of gratitude, and positive relationships with others as a worthy starting point. "A" in the iNEAR brings forth the liberating power of awareness and of freedom "to be the person that we are / to become the person that we can be". Inbar understood the notion of the freedom of the will in relation to both the human condition and God. This understanding allowed her to unlock opportunities for grasping her struggles, wishes, and needs through the lens of the existential responsibility to own our freedom as a way of being *recognised*, as a way of being *seen* and *valued* by oneself, by others, and by divinity. Its implications are far reaching and include "big" and ordinary choices. It also includes preoccupations with how we make sense of, how we (re)frame, and how we respond to everyday emotional experiences; here, for instance, Inbar found beneficial conversations about the emergence and use of emotions in line with an Islamic intention to observe a lifestyle of compassion, honesty, and deliberate harmony. Finally, "R", "responding with growth in spite of ...", positions resilience as a valuable response to life and lifestyle challenges wherein the potential can become actualised. Inbar emphasised "What I *share* with others" to be, for her, crucial for the capacity to be resilient alongside "What I am and what I can". In doing so Inbar is showcasing the Western concept of community and the Islamic view of wholeness as potentially entangled and complementary. The coaching sessions which were structured through the lens of iNEAR also involved themed activities that held an inspirational and/or transitional place for Inbar between and within our sessions. For instance, Inbar would bring a quote from Rumi or Al-Ghazali to reflect her understanding of what is being discussed and processed—for instance, "Yesterday I was clever, so I wanted to change the world. Today I am wise, so I am changing myself" (Rumi).

Through narration, systematic examination, and at times brave introspection, coaching dialogues can reveal the dominant and competing discourses available to us to build self-representations across personal, social, and professional contexts. As anticipated, coaching processes involving structured advice, guided explorations, and co-authored alternative narratives can facilitate a client's efforts to arrive at positive negotiations of lifestyle dilemmas and realise optimal functioning in professional or personal contexts. However, the coaching work with Inbar highlights a further crucial and exciting aspect of coaching in Islamic contexts. It highlights the existential and potentially transformative nature of the Islamic philosophy, value systems, and practice. It makes obvious how the choices we make to conduct our daily life are complexly constitutive of self-identity. It makes obvious how potential selves get imagined and rehearsed through the coaching relationship. It makes obvious how change is always already discursive and existential in nature.

Practical implications

- Coaches working in an Islamic context should hold basic knowledge of Islamic philosophy, values, and practice
- Coaches should be clear about the coaching aim as separate from imparting or clarifying Islamic teaching
- Coaches can work with coachees to develop their views on the importance of forging congruence between the Islamic philosophy, values, and practice and the professional lifestyle, demands, and choices.

Brief biographical information

Dr Aneta D. Tunariu is a chartered psychologist with the British Psychological Society, principal lecturer in psychology with specialism in the psychology of relationships, and the head of subject for psychological interventions in the School of Psychology, University of East London, UK. Her applied coaching practice, academic expertise, and research are closely informed by concepts from existential positive psychology, coaching psychology, developmental psychoanalytic theory, and psychotherapy. Dr Tunariu offers practitioner-oriented workshops, keynote lectures, and research presentations in both national and international settings, and is regularly commissioned to deliver bespoke psychological interventions across the private and public sectors.

* * *

Personal stories

In addition to the broad range of case studies provided above, we thought it would be helpful to share two pertinent personal stories. Both of these stories demonstrate how powerful and transformative it can be to learn about coaching and then coach others.

In the first personal story, one of the authors of this book reflects on the use of coaching with leaders and executives in private and government organisations covering various aspects of leadership, behaviour, emotional intelligence, and communication in Islamic culture.

Personal story: A journey of curiosity, learning, and growth

Author: Raja'a Yousif Allaho—accredited certified coach and mentor coach, International Coach Federation, Kuwait & Gulf

I started my career in consulting and training in 2001 after a long work experience in the government sector in planning and development. I have always found my passion in working with people and providing some added value. This was inspired by the quote of the Prophet Muhammad (peace be upon him): "Be as a birthmark." This means being unique in my perspective and my work, always asking myself what unique role I could play that would add value to myself and others as a way of presenting my Islamic personality.

In 2007, I attended a certification programme to be trained as a trainer in a customer service programme. The topic was "coaching for stellar services" and this was the first time that I had heard about the word "coaching". At that moment, I felt that I had found what I was looking for. It was the answer to my own question about the role in life that God had created for me. That is when I started my coaching journey with passion, fear, and curiosity. I decided to take the professional route in learning and practising coaching, as it was still a relatively new concept. I searched for a reliable source for learning and attended a foundation coaching programme in the UK in January 2008. My goal was to gain learning and knowledge and to be a professional in this area. Throughout the training programme, I was curious about the following questions:

- Is coaching what I am looking for?
- How would it be possible to present this concept in the Gulf region?
- Is it compatible with our culture?
- Is this a new concept?
- How will I support people by applying this concept?
- What is the added value element in this concept?

On the last day of the programme, the facilitator asked each participant to create an "elevator pitch" when introducing themselves as a coach. I said my role was to "support you to lead yourself and others". In that moment I decided that my role in life was to support people to be genuine human beings by leading themselves (first) and others, working in collaboration with managers and executives. That was a real moment of "shift" in my life. When I returned home, I spent most of my time reading, researching, thinking, finding answers to all the questions raised during the training programme. I then joined the International Coach Federation (ICF) to introduce myself to the global coaching community and became the first Arab accredited coach in Kuwait. I added Arabic to ICF as a coaching language. I continued to work hard with passion in marketing and learning coaching and realised the following:

• Coaching is a concept that has been known and practised in Islamic culture over the last 700 years.
• Muslim professionals in psychology wrote books regarding "guidance" in Islamic culture. These books covered some of the key skills and practices used by coaches today.
• Coaching practices will be more powerful when they take into consideration Islamic beliefs and ethics.
• The need to design a coaching curriculum combining Islamic beliefs, values, and culture with international knowledge and expertise using the Arabic language.
• The need to promote the concept in the Gulf region through regular coaching conferences.

This led to further investigation, reading about coaching, mentoring, and guidance in Arab and Islamic culture. I attended classes to learn about interpretation of the Noble Qur'an as this text provides Muslims with information, answers, and solutions to all aspects of our lives. During this process, I found further answers for all the questions that I had been thinking about deeply during and after completing my coach training.

I designed and developed coaching practices and tools to cover Islamic beliefs and values, supporting my clients to achieve the following:

• Clarification and strengthening of their beliefs followed by appropriate actions
• Alignment and integrity in all aspects of life
• Creation of awareness regarding their role in life
• Reinforcement of personal confidence and self-esteem.

The tools and practices that I applied in my coaching are:

• Emphasising my client's beliefs in order to raise awareness. When my clients faced situations in their work or life that they felt were unfair, or raised worries about their future, I would ask them, "Who can hurt you?" Muslims would answer with "No one but God." When clients became confident about this and their beliefs, I would then ask, "Therefore, how will you practise your belief in this situation?" This can be a powerful way of connecting clients to their existing beliefs.

- Working with human alignment. I would support my clients to achieve integrity by coaching them around their relationships using the Alignment Wheel to ask questions about their relationships with God, self, life, and others.

- Focusing on areas of strength. We usually forget our areas of strength and unique capabilities when we get "busy" in life. According to Islamic belief, each person is created for a specific role in his or her life in order to cooperate with others to build the universe (e'maar). This reminder can help clients to build self-confidence and acceptance.

- Islam focuses on and rewards the practising and applying of ethics in our daily interactions. I take this into consideration while coaching my clients to help them to measure or evaluate their actions and behaviours according to the Islamic code of ethics.

- I use coaching to motivate my clients to learn and read which was the first call from God to Prophet Muhammad (peace be upon him). Reading and learning are important tools for human development.

- In Islam each person is responsible for his or her actions. I provide coaching support to my coachees by encouraging them to be more responsible by taking on new initiatives and developing and correcting issues around them.

Practical implications

- Religion and beliefs are essential in achieving human integrity.
- The Noble Qur'an is a complete methodology for a Muslim's life. We cannot separate personal actions without reference to Qur'anic instruction. Many challenges faced by people are a result of this separation.
- Coaches who are willing to practise coaching in Islamic culture need to take into consideration the ideas, concepts, and practices presented in this book.

This final case study presents a moving personal story in which the author explains the impact that coaching has had on her personal and professional life.

Personal story: A journey of discovery

Author: Rania Shamas, senior vice president, leading commercial
   organisation, UAE

I started within my current organisation as a store supervisor in 1999. By 2012, I had progressed to become the general manager of retail operations. During my busy professional life, I didn't have much time to reflect on my own personal and professional development. I considered myself successful and did not ask too many questions! However, my life changed completely when I was blessed with a new baby girl on 28 October 2012.

Myriam was different to any other child. She is very unique in that you really need to be as open as her heart to communicate with her at the level she is in! That moment was a reality check for me. I realised that I knew very little about life, becoming aware that I needed to escalate myself, in mind, heart, and soul. At that time, our internal coach supported me to look inwards and understand myself better. During one coaching conversation, we decided that I would write a positive learning journal about my experiences with Myriam. This powerful conversation made me interested in becoming a coach, and I ended up registering on a coaching course. The wonderful learning journal about Myriam became the basis for my coaching journal. As I spent time learning and reflecting, the magic began. I started to reflect on my life stories—and was able to see things from a variety of perspectives.

At one point, I became concerned that the insights emerging out of the coaching course would negatively impact my beliefs and faith—but it had the opposite effect. I was able to see Islamic teaching and values in almost every coaching scenario. Very important Islamic concepts such as trust, helping others, empathy, belief, being genuine, having a life purpose, wisdom, and humanity were also evident in coaching.

I was able to connect some of the coaching principles with ideas from the Hadith:

• We should have a clear intention
• We should sit properly and close to the speaker

- We should ask short and good questions to gain better understanding
- We should seek knowledge from the right authority and source
- We should maintain good listening skills.

I had never understood my religion the way I did after learning about coaching. It is about being with a person, mirroring his or her view, reminding them of their life purpose and the good qualities he or she has. We, as individuals, can change the world with our support to each other. Coaching has brought me back to life through confidence and love. Through being coached and coaching others, I have become the person I am today: a proud mother and an inspirational leader. I am now a proud mother of three amazing girls, a wife of a kind-hearted entrepreneur, a senior vice president for a prestigious retailer, a professional life coach, and executive coach. The secret was growing myself!

I feel it is my duty is to share my experience and help people to grow and evolve (my life purpose had appeared to be still in draft mode). This energy drove me towards taking a more responsible role to mentor and coach individuals who wanted to achieve more for themselves. In this part of the world, most of our families taught us to close up, when coaching is all about opening up. We were told not to trust others, when coaching explains the importance of trust. We were told to get perfect scores in our exams, when coaching tells you it is OK to fail because that is how you learn and grow.

In one coaching conversation, I was working with a Muslim who was raised to believe that you should only complain to God. As a result of the coaching she read the Hadith Shareef (Al-Tirmidhi Hadith 249, narrated by Al-Hasan al-Basri): God's Messenger (peace be upon him) said: "He whom death overtakes while he is engaged in acquiring knowledge with a view to reviving Islam with the help of it, there will be one degree between him and the Prophets in Paradise." It was a beautiful discovery for both of us. Coaches learn from their coachees the same way coachees learn. It is like a symphony in that you come out of it more self-aware and enthusiastic towards your life journey. Another coachee was always reacting badly to people and situations. When I asked her who was reacting, she realised that evil might be taking over in those moments. What a beautiful realisation to know that inside us we have the wisdom to act kindly even when evil tries to take over the theatre of our life!

I am humbled and honoured to have the opportunity to share my story with you.

REFERENCES

Abbas & Mohammed (2009), quoted in Al Jaboori (2014), *Education and Counseling in Islam*. Amman: Dar Al Hamed.

Abu Ghazaleh (1978), quoted in Al Jaboori (2014), *Education and Counseling in Islam*. Amman: Dar Al Hamed.

Al-Ani (2000), quoted in Al Jaboori (2014), *Education and Counseling in Islam*. Amman: Dar.

Al-Hayani (1989), quoted in Al Jaboori (2014), *Education and Counseling in Islam*. Amman: Dar Al Hamed.

Al-Isawi, A. (1992). *Islamic and Scientific Guidance and Mentoring*. Beirut: Dar al Nahda al Arabiyyah.

Al Jaboori, A. (2014). *Education and Counseling in Islam*. Amman: Dar Al Hamed.

Al-Kayali, M. (2008). *Philosophy of Islamic Education*. Dubai: Dar Al Galam.

Al-Khatib (2004), quoted in Al Jaboori (2014), *Education and Counseling in Islam*. Amman: Dar Al Hamed.

Al-Marsafi, S. (2008). *Characteristic of the Center Nation's Culture*. Kuwait: International Islamic Charity Organization.

Al-Mighmasy (1993), quoted in Al Jaboori (2014), *Education and Counseling in Islam*. Amman: Dar Al Hamed.

Al-Sayyid (1997), quoted in Al Jaboori (2014), *Education and Counseling in Islam*. Amman: Dar Al Hamed.

145

Al-Zubeidi, A. (2008). *Foundations of guiding and directing from Islamic education's perspective*. Mecca: Um Al Qura University.

Arberry, A. J. (1955). *The Koran Interpreted*. New York: Macmillan.

Bachkirova, T., Cox, E., & Clutterbuck, D. (2014). Introduction. In: E. Cox, T. Bachkirova, and D. Clutterbuck (Eds.), *The Complete Handbook of Coaching (2nd edn.)* (pp. 1–18). London: Sage.

Day, D., & Carpenter, T. (2016). *A History of Sports Coaching in Britain: Overcoming Amateurism*. London: Routledge.

de Haan, E. (2008). *Relational Coaching: Journeys towards Mastering One to One Learning*. Chichester, UK: Wiley.

Downey, M. (2003). *Effective Coaching: Lessons from the Coach's Coach (2nd edn.)*. London: Texere.

Fredrickson, B. L., & Losada, M. F. (2005). Positive affect and the complex dynamics of human flourishing. *American Psychologist, 60*(7): 678–686.

Gallwey, W. T. (1974). *The Inner Game of Tennis*. New York: Random House.

GEMS Learning Gateway. https://www.gemslearninggateway.com. CharacteristicsofEthicalTeaching (accessed 13 August 2016).

Grant, A. M., Passmore, J., Cavanagh, M., & Parker, H. M. (2010). The state of play in coaching today: A comprehensive review of the field. *International Review of Industrial and Organizational Psychology, 25*(1): 125–167.

Grencavage, L., & Norcross, J. (1990). Where are the commonalities among the therapeutic common factors? *Professional Psychology: Research and Practice, 21*(5): 372–378.

Ibn-Tamiyya (2008), quoted in Al-Zubeidi, A. *Foundations of guiding and directing from Islamic education's perspective*. Master's thesis. Mecca: Um Al Qura University.

Kline, N. (1999). *Time to Think: Listening to Ignite the Human Mind*. London: Cassell.

Knight, J. (2007). *Instructional Coaching: A Partnership Approach to Improving Instruction*. Thousand Oaks, CA: Corwin.

Knight, J. (2014). *Focus on Teaching: Using Video for High-impact Instruction*. Thousand Oaks, CA: Corwin.

Mahmoud (1998), quoted in Al Jaboori (2014), *Education and Counseling in Islam*. Amman: Dar Al Hamed.

Mann, C. (2016). *6th Ridler Report: Strategic Trends in the Use of Coaching*. London: Ridler.

Omar (1984), quoted in Al Jaboori (2014), *Education and Counseling in Islam*. Amman: Dar Al Hamed.

Online Etymology Dictionary. http://www.etymonline.com/index.php?term=coach (accessed 25 March 2016).

Palmer, T., & Arnold, V. (2009). Coaching in the Middle East. In: J. Passmore (Ed.), *Diversity in Coaching*. London: Kogan Page.

Passmore, J. (Ed.) (2008). *Psychometrics in Coaching: Using Psychological and Psychometric Tools for Development*. London: Kogan Page.

Passmore, J., & Fillery-Travis, A. (2011). A critical review of executive coaching research: A decade of progress and what's to come. *Coaching: An International Journal of Theory, Research and Practice*, 4(2): 70–88.

Passmore, J., & Theeboom, T. (2015). Coaching psychology: A journey of development in research. In: L. E. van Zyl, M. W. Stander, & A. Oodendal (Eds.), *Coaching Psychology: Meta-theoretical Perspectives and Applications in Multi-cultural Contexts*. New York: Springer.

Pease, A., & Pease, B. (2005). *The Definitive Book of Body Language*. London: Orion.

Qutb, S. (1996). *Fi Zilal al-Qur'an*. Beirut: Dar al-Shuruq.

Rogers, C. R. (1980). *A Way of Being*. Boston, MA: Houghton Mifflin.

Rosinski, P. (2003). *Coaching across Cultures*. London: Nicholas Brealey.

Sherpa Coaching (2015). *Executive Coaching Survey: Full Report*. Cincinnati, OH: Sherpa Coaching.

Theeboom, T. (2016). The current state of the research. In: C. van Nieuwerburgh (Ed.), *Coaching in Professional Contexts* (pp. 187–197). London: Sage.

Theeboom, T., Beersma, B., & van Vianen, A. E. (2014). Does coaching work: A meta-analysis on the effects of coaching on individual level outcomes in an organizational context. *Journal of Positive Psychology*, 9(1): 1–18.

Tunariu, A. D. (2015). *iNEAR—a Resilience Curriculum Programme for Children and Young People*. Teacher and Student Guides & Research Evaluation Report. London: University of East London.

Tunariu, A. D. (2017). *iNEAR—a Culturally Adapted Coaching and Positive Psychology Programme for Resilience and Well-being in the Context of Dual Cultural Heritage*. Trainer guide and delivery materials. London: University of East London.

Tunariu, A. D., & El Guenuni, F. (2016). Towards Resilient and Positive Identities. A three-day training programme delivered for and in collaboration with The Raihan Charity, Larache, Morocco.

van Nieuwerburgh, C. (Ed.) (2012). *Coaching in Education: Getting Better Results for Students, Educators and Parents*. London: Karnac.

van Nieuwerburgh, C. (2017). *An Introduction to Coaching Skills: A Practical Guide (2nd edn.)*. London: Sage.

van Nieuwerburgh, C. (Ed.) (2016). *Coaching in Professional Contexts*. London: Sage.

van Nieuwerburgh, C., & Barr, M. (2016). Coaching in education. In: T. Bachkirova, G. Spence, & D. Drake (Eds.), *The Sage Handbook of Coaching*. London: Sage.

Whitmore, J. (1992). *Coaching for Performance: A Practical Guide to Growing Your Own Skills*. London: Nicholas Brealey.

Whitmore, J. (2009). *Coaching for Performance: GROWing Human Potential and Purpose: The Principles and Practice of Coaching and Leading* (4th edn.). London: Nicholas Brealey.

Zahran (1980), quoted in Al Jaboori (2014), *Education and Counseling in Islam.* Amman: Dar Al Hamed.

INDEX

Abbas, Ibn, 17, 81
Abu Ghazaleh, 16
Abu Hamid al-Ghazali, 70
Al-Ani, 17
Al-Bukhari, 12
Al-Hayani, 16
Alignment Wheel, 86, 89, 97, 102, 114
    see also: Ershad coaching
        framework
  assured self, 95–97
  bad deed's self, 94
  balancing factors in Islam, 93
  blaming self, 95
  coaching and spirituality, 92
  facilitator, 100, 101
  human self, 91, 94
  law of *taskheer*, 100
  relationships, 97
  relationship with beliefs, 98–99
  relationship with life, 100–101
  relationship with other people,
    101–102
  relationship with self, 99–100

  role of, 114
  self in Noble Qur'an, 93–94
  spiritual dimension, 90–92
  worship, 98
Al-Isawi, A., 16
Al-Kayali, M., 69
Al-Khatib, 16
Al-Marsafi, S., 9
Al-Mighmasy, 16
Al-Sayyid, 17
Al-Zubeidi, A., 89
American Psychological Association
    (APA), 5
Arberry, A. J., xxiv
Arnold, V., xxiii
ar-rushd, xxv
assured self, 93, 95–97 *see also*:
    Alignment Wheel
Australian Psychological Society
    (APS), 5

Bachkirova, T., 6
balance, 14–15 *see also*: Islamic culture

Barr, M., 116, 130
Beersma, B., 116
body language clues, 30–31 *see also*:
    listening with purpose
British Psychological Society (BPS), 5

Carpenter, T., 2
case studies, 117 *see also*: personal
    stories
    educational coaching, 130–134
    one-to-one coaching, 135–138
    professional coaching, 117
Cavanagh, M., 116
Charmaine, 123
closed questions, 39–40 *see also*:
    questions
Clutterbuck, D., 6
coach, 2, 19–20 *see also*: Islamic culture
    key skills, 47
    responsibilities of, 67
    vs. teachers, and preachers, 18
coachee, xxiv, 7
    body language, 30–31
    increasing self-awareness, 23–25
    valuing, 25–26
coaching, xxi, 5–6, 67 *see also*: Ershad
    coaching facilitators; Ershad
    coaching framework;
    partnership principles
    balanced view of, xxiii
    and consultancy, 8
    conversations, 67
    and counselling, 7
    culturally appropriate approach,
        xxiii
    different views about, 6
    Iqra, xxvi
    Kuwaiti Coaching Conference, xxiv
    and mentoring, 7
    Noble Qur'an, xxiv–xxvi
    passion for, xxii
    research into, 5
    skills, 112–113
    and spirituality, 92
    strategies, xxii–xxiii

    way of being, 103
coaching, history of, 1, 8
    academic field, 4–5
    ancient Greece, 1
    business, 2–3
    coach, 2
    experience of executive coaching, 8
    humanistic psychology, 3
    Hungarian town, 2
    inner game, 3
    professional contexts, 4
    research into coaching, 5
    sources of executive coaching, 4
    sports coaching, 2
    University of Oxford, 2
coaching in educational contexts,
        130–134 *see also*: case studies
    supporting executive education
        student, 132–134
    third culture spaces, 130–132
coaching in professional contexts, 117
        see also: case studies; Ershad
        coaching framework
    Gulf national in university context,
        118–120
    ihsan, 123–127
    UAE nationals in leadership
        positions, 120–123
    Western coaches and Saudi Arabian
        clients, 127–130
consultancy, 8
conversational process, 112–114
    coaching skills, 112–113
    phases of, 113
cooperation, 101
counselling, 7
Cox, E., 6

Day, D., 2
de Haan, E., 6, 27
Downey, M., 6

effective coaching elements, 109
El Guenuni, F., 135
E'maar, 68, 69–71

Ershad coaching, xxiii–xxiv, xxvi, 68, 111
Ershad coaching facilitators *see also*: partnership principles
  belief in learner ability, 106
  caring about people, 107
  compassion and gentleness, 108
  humanity, 108
  humility, 106
  integrity, 107
  patience, 108
  practical implications for, 108–110
  respectful approach, 107
  self-confidence, 106
  three elements of effective coaching, 109
Ershad coaching framework, 67, 111
  Abu Hamid al-Ghazali and theory of science, 70
  Alignment Wheel, 86, 114
  authors, 114–115
  coaching skills, 112–113
  coach's role, 71
  components, 112
  contracting, 68
  conversational process, 112–114
  discovery, 78–80
  effective facilitators, 113
  effort, 86–88
  E'maar, 69–71
  Ershad coaching conversation, 78
  facilitator, 72–73, 116
  facilitator's role in building partnership conditions, 74
  intangible and tangible actions, 80–81
  integrated coaching model, 71
  intention, 80–84, 85
  learner's role in building partnership conditions, 75
  looking forward, 116
  partnership conditions, 71, 72, 112
  pathways, 84–86
  purpose of human beings, 68
  respect in Islam, 75–78

  review of, 112
  self-esteem, 76
  sincerity, 81–82
  tangible benefits to learners, 109–110
  typical coaching conversation, 67
  worshipping of god, 69
executive coaching, 4 *see also*: coaching
  experience of, 8
  sources, 4

facilitator, 72 *see also*: Ershad coaching facilitators; Ershad coaching framework
  Alignment Wheel, 100, 101
  effective, 113
  of Ershad coaching, 116
  questions by, 79, 83, 85, 87
  role in building partnership conditions, 74
feedback, 57
  based on questionnaires or evaluations, 60
  about coaching conversation, 60
  difficulty in giving and receiving, 57–58
  giving feedback following observation, 61–62
  negative feedback, 57
  provided by coach, 58–61
  providing clear and specific, 63–64
  recipient, 59
  sugarcoating negative feedback
  360 degree questionnaire, 61
  tips about giving feedback, 63–64
  tips about receiving feedback, 64–65
  watered-down feedback, 63
Fillery-Travis, A., 5, 116
Fredrickson, B. L., 64

Gallwey, W. T., 3
governance, 100
Grant, A. M., 116
Grencavage, L., 27

GROW model, 3
guidance, 16–17 *see also*: Islamic culture
gymnasts, 1

hearing, 34 *see also*: listening with
      purpose
human configuration, 91
Human Potential Movement, 3
human self, 94
humility, 106

Ibn Abbas, 81
Ibn-Taymiyya, 90
inner game, 3
intangible and tangible actions, 80–81
      see also: Ershad coaching
      framework
Iqra, xxvi
Islam, 89
      spiritual education of, 90
Islamic culture, 9
      balance, 14–15
      characteristics of, 10
      coach, 19–20
      comprehensiveness, 12
      constancy, 11–12
      divinity, 10–11
      guidance, 16–17
      mentoring in Islam, 16–17
      positivity, 12–13
      preacher, 19
      realism, 13–14
      teacher, 17–19

Kline, N., 22, 27
Knight, J., 62, 103
kocsi, 2
Kuwaiti Coaching Conference, xxiv

leading questions, 40–41 *see also*:
      questions
learning purpose, 89
listening with purpose, 21, 36
      being comfortable with not
            knowing, 33–34
      body language, 29

body language clues, 30–31
building trust, 27
concept of listening in Noble
      Qur'an, 34–36
creating thinking space, 27
energy levels, 31–32
eye contact, 29
increasing self-awareness of
      coachee, 23–25
listening to coaches, 23
maintaining non-judgmental
      stance, 32–33
power of listening, 21–22
practical skills, 27–34
purpose of coaching, 22
reducing amount of time speaking,
      28
reducing distractions, 34
remembering purposes of listening,
      28–29
showing interest in topic being
      discussed, 26
silences and quiet moments, 32
transformational conversation, 21
valuing coachee, 25–26
withholding advice, 33
Losada, M. F., 64

Mahmoud, 16
making civilization *see* E'maar
Maslow, A., 3
mentor, 1
mentoring, 7
Mohammed, 17
multiple questions, 41–42 *see also*:
      questions
Muslim, 89
      building character, 90
      cooperation, 101
      healthy self of, 99–100

Noble Qur'an, xxiv–xxvi, 70
      advantages of moderation, 90–92
      ar-rushd, xxv
      concept of listening in, 34–36
      human configuration, 91

self in, 93–94
status of questions in, 44
Norcross, J., 27

Odyssey, The, 1
Omar, 16
one-to-one coaching, 135–138 *see also*:
    case studies
open questions, 38–39 *see also*:
    questions

Palmer, T., xxiii
paraphrasing, 47 *see also*: summarising
    features, 48
    and mirroring, 49–50
    and summarising when coaching,
        56
    when coaching, 48–50
Parker, H. M., 116
partnership conditions, 71, 72, 112
        see also: Ershad coaching
        framework
partnership principles, 103 *see also*:
        Ershad coaching facilitators
    choice, 104
    dialogue, 104
    equality, 104
    praxis, 104–105
    reciprocity, 105
    reflection, 105
    voice, 105
Passmore, J., 5, 60, 116
Pease, A., 30
Pease, B., 30
personal stories, 138–143 *see also*:
        case studies
    coaching impact, 142–143
    coaching with leaders and
        executives, 139–141
preacher, 19 *see also*: Islamic culture
    vs. teachers, and coaches, 18

questions, 37
    closed, 39–40
    in coaching, 37
    Hadith, 45

importance in Sunnah, 45
leading, 40–41
multiple, 41–42
open, 38–39
purpose of, 42–44
status in Noble Qur'an, 44
types of, 37
Qutb, S., 95

relationship *see also*: Alignment Wheel
    with beliefs, 98–99
    with life, 100–101
    with other people, 101–102
    with self, 99–100
religious aspect, 69
respect, 75 *see also*: Ershad coaching
        framework
    for leaders, 77
    for non-Muslims, 78
    for parents, 76
    for scholars and scientists, 77
    self-esteem, 76
    for women, 76
    for young and old, 77
Rogers, C. R., 3, 105
Rosinski, P., 6

scales, 14
self, 99
self-esteem, 76 *see also*: Ershad coaching
        framework
social aspect, 69
spiritual dimension, 90–92 *see also*:
        Alignment Wheel
sports coaching, 2
sugarcoating, 63 *see also*: feedback
summarising, 47 *see also*: paraphrasing
    features, 48
    outcomes, 50
    and paraphrasing when coaching,
        56
    when coaching, 50–56

talent development centre (TDC),
        120–121
taskheer law, 100

tawjih, xxiv
teacher, 17–19 *see also*: Islamic culture
    vs. preachers, and coaches, 18
Theeboom, T., 5, 116
360 degree survey, 61 *see also*: feedback
transformational conversation, 21
        see also: listening with
        purpose
Tunariu, A. D., 135

universal aspect, 69

van Nieuwerburgh, C., xxviii, 4, 6,
    19, 30–31, 37, 57, 63, 105, 107,
    110, 116, 117, 130
van Vianen, A. E., 116

way of being, 105
Whitmore, J., 6
worship, 98
worshipping of god, 69

Zahran, 16

For Product Safety Concerns and Information please contact our EU
representative GPSR@taylorandfrancis.com
Taylor & Francis Verlag GmbH, Kaufingerstraße 24, 80331 München, Germany

www.ingramcontent.com/pod-product-compliance
Lightning Source LLC
Chambersburg PA
CBHW070339270326
41926CB00017B/3920

9 781782 201991